A VISUAL ENCYCLOPEDIA OF
AMERICAN
PRESIDENTS
1789–1901

A VISUAL ENCYCLOPEDIA OF
AMERICAN PRESIDENTS
1789–1901

A chronological guide to more than a century of
American presidents, from George Washington to
William McKinley, with an analysis of the role of each
as president, statesman and private individual

PROFESSOR JON ROPER

southwater

This edition is published by Southwater
an imprint of Anness Publishing Ltd
Blaby Road, Wigston
Leicestershire LE18 4SE
info@anness.com

www.southwaterbooks.com; www.annesspublishing.com

Anness Publishing has a new picture agency outlet for images for publishing, promotions
or advertising. Please visit our website www.practicalpictures.com for more information.

Publisher: Joanna Lorenz
Editorial Director: Helen Sudell
Project Editor: Simona Hill
Designer: Nigel Partridge
All state flags illustrated by Alfred Znamierowski
All maps illustrated by Tom Connell
Production Controller: Christine Ni

Previously published as part of a larger volume *The Illustrated Encyclopedia of
the Presidents of America*

PUBLISHER'S NOTE
Although the advice and information in this book are believed to be accurate
and true at the time of going to press, neither the authors nor the publisher can accept
any legal responsibility or liability for any errors or omissions that may be made.

PICTURE CREDITS
Peter Newark's American Pictures: 1, 22, 23 top, 28, 31, 35, 44, 48, 49, 50, 52 top,
54 bottom, 56, 63 bottom right, 64, 68, 72, 74, 75, 92. THE BRIDGEMAN ART LIBRARY:
Page 4 second from bottom, 30, 34, top, 36,66, 72 top, 80 bottom, 82–3, 90, 97 bottom,
98, 99 both, 102, 104 bottom, 113 top left and bottom, 115 all. ALAMY: 4 second from
top, 6 top, 9 top, 21 bottom, 25, 27, 37 bottom, 42–3, 43 bottom, 47 left, 53 top, 81 top,
103 left, 122 top, 126 bottom. NORTHWIND PICTURE ARCHIVE: 52 bottom, 54 top,
55 bottom. CORBIS: 2, 3, 4 top, middle bottom, 5 all, 6 bottom, 7 both, 8 both, 9 bottom
(both), 10–11, 12–13, 14 bottom, 15 both, 16 both, 17, 20, 21 top, 23 bottom, 24, 25 top,
26, 29, 32, 33, 34 bottom, 37 top, 40, 41, 42 top, 43 top, 45 both, 46 bottom, 47 top right
and bottom, 49 bottom, 51 right, 53 bottom, 55 top, 58 left, 59 both, 60–1, 63 top middle, top right, bottom middle, 65, 69 both, 70 both, 71 top, 73 , 76, 77, 78 top, 79 top, 80
top, 84, 85, 86, 87, 88, 89, 90 top, 93, 94 both, 95, 96 both, 97 top, 100, 101, 103 bottom
right, 104 right, 105, 106–7, 108 both, 109 both, 110 both, 111, 112, 113 top right, 114
both, 116, 117 top, 118, 119, 120, 121 both, 122, 124, 125 both, 126 left, 127 all, 128 all.
GETTY IMAGES: 67 top.

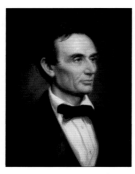

ETHICAL TRADING POLICY
Because of our ongoing ecological investment programme, you, as our customer, can
have the pleasure and reassurance of knowing that a tree is being cultivated on your
behalf to naturally replace the materials used to make the book you are holding.
For further information about this scheme, go to www.annesspublishing.com/trees

Page 1 George Washington, Page 2 Framing the Constitution, Page 3 The White House,
Page 4 top to bottom: Capitol Hill, John Adams, Supreme Court, Abraham Lincoln,
Mount Rushmore, Page 5 top to bottom: The Declaration of Independence, The
Opening of the White House, The War of 1812, The Battle of Gettysburg, The Meeting
of the Railways at Utah.

CONTENTS

INTRODUCTION

The president of the USA is the world's most powerful political leader, a fact that George Washington, the country's first president, could never have envisaged when he took office more than 200 years ago. Washington is ranked as one of the greatest presidents to have served his country, but few of his successors have soared to such an iconic stature.

Beginning with a history of the key events that led to the formation of a new nation, this book presents a chronological account of the 25 statesmen who have held high office from 1789 to 1901. Each is presented along with an objective assessment of their background and their lasting legacy, and is set within the context of key domestic, social and political events.

Below: George Washington sees the first American flag made by Betsy Ross.

While the names of George Washington, Thomas Jefferson and Abraham Lincoln still resonate in the nation's history, others, such as Millard Fillmore, Franklin Pierce, Chester Arthur and Benjamin Harrison have drifted into obscurity. John Quincy Adams and Rutherford B. Hayes are remembered more for the controversial circumstances of their election than for their achievements in office. History pays scant attention to the legacy of many presidents.

James Madison, the architect of the United States Constitution, believed that is how it should be: executive power invested in the president in America's republican government was best checked, balanced and contained by other institutions of government, such as the Supreme Court and the houses of Congress. The presidency was

Above: The bald eagle became the national symbol in 1782, during the American War of Independence.

never intended to be the focal point of the political system. Neither was the vice-presidential office to be a stepping stone to winning the presidency. Between 1788 and 1900 John Adams and Martin Van Buren were the only vice presidents to fulfil that ambition.

By refusing to hold on to office for longer than eight years, George Washington established an important precedent for his successors, most of whom felt constrained by his example. Yet his self-imposed limit proved more of an aspiration than an achievement. Only six presidents elected in the 19th century completed eight years in office. Two more – Lincoln and William McKinley – were re-elected to a second term, but both were assassinated soon afterwards. James Polk was the first to retire voluntarily after four years in the White House, becoming one of the seven 19th-century presidents who completed only a single term.

Until the Civil War (1861–5), presidents struggled to keep the United States together in the face of sectional tensions, such as those caused by the

Above: The White House has been the President's official purpose-built residence since 1800.

issue of slavery that threatened to tear it apart. Of the 14 presidents preceding James Buchanan, who left office in the year the war broke out, nine came from the slave-holding South. After the war ended, for the remainder of the century, nobody from the former Confederate States ran for executive office. At the

same time, President Ulysses S. Grant and his successors surveyed a new and challenging political landscape as America experienced a period of rapid economic and social change.

Alongside an analysis of the presidents, this fascinating volume provides an insight into the developing social and political history of the United States, from the War of Independence, to westward expansion, slavery, the Civil War, and Reconstruction.

PRESIDENTIAL ROLL CALL TO 1901

George Washington, 1789–1797	Franklin Pierce, 1853–1857
John Adams, 1797–1801	James Buchanan, 1857–1861
Thomas Jefferson, 1801–1809	Abraham Lincoln, 1861–1865
James Madison, 1809–1817	Andrew Johnson, 1865–1869
James Monroe, 1817–1825	Ulysses S. Grant, 1869–1877
John Quincy Adams, 1825–1829	Rutherford Hayes, 1877–1881
Andrew Jackson, 1829–1837	James Garfield, 1881
Martin Van Buren, 1837–1841	Chester Arthur, 1881–1885
William Henry Harrison, 1841	Grover Cleveland, 1885–1889
John Tyler, 1841–1845	Benjamin Harrison, 1889–1893
James Polk, 1845–1849	Grover Cleveland (again), 1893–1897
Zachary Taylor, 1849–1850	William McKinley, 1897–1901
Millard Fillmore, 1850–1853	

CHAPTER ONE

GEORGE WASHINGTON, JOHN ADAMS

AND THE FOUNDING OF THE UNITED STATES OF AMERICA, 1754–1801

THE AMERICAN REVOLUTION HAD COMPLEX CAUSES, BUT ITS CHIEF RESULT WAS THE SETTING UP OF THE WORLD'S FIRST SUCCESSFUL FEDERAL GOVERNMENT. AT THE TIME OF THE FIRST CONTINENTAL CONGRESS IN 1775, NONE OF THE PARTICIPANTS KNEW WHAT FORM THEIR NEW CONSTITUTION WOULD TAKE, SHOULD THEIR STRUGGLE AGAINST THE BRITISH BE SUCCESSFUL, BUT THEY KNEW THAT IT MUST BE BASED ON A NEW SET OF PRINCIPLES. THE COLONISTS' DISCONTENT HAD BECOME FOCUSED ON THE MONARCHY, AND THEY WERE SETTING OUT TO REJECT NOT JUST BRITISH RULE BUT ALSO THE BRITISH PATTERN OF GOVERNMENT. THE CONSTITUTION AGREED IN PHILADELPHIA IN 1787 WAS DESIGNED TO PREVENT THE ACCESSION OF AN AUTOCRAT IN THE MANNER OF THE BRITISH MONARCH. THE SOLUTION LAY IN THE ELECTION OF A PRESIDENT WITH EXECUTIVE AUTHORITY, HELD IN CHECK BY THE JUDICIAL AND LEGISLATIVE BRANCHES OF THE GOVERNMENT.

Left: The Declaration of Independence (1776) was part of a revolution that paved the way for the Federal Constitution (1787).

THE ROAD TO REBELLION
1754–1775

What were the events that turned the man who would become the first president of the United States into a rebel? George Washington began his military career fighting alongside the British to prevent the French settlers from encroaching upon land in the Ohio Territory west of Virginia. He ended it against all odds as the general who forced Britain to give up its North American colonies. Along the way, he hastened the course of history.

In 1754, as a freshly promoted lieutenant colonel in the Virginia regiment, the 22-year-old Washington ordered his men to fire on a detachment of French forces. It proved to be the first engagement in what escalated into the French and Indian War. The following year he returned to the Ohio Territory with Major-General Edward Braddock, the commander-in-chief of British forces in America. This time he experienced a heavy defeat at the hands of the French defending the strategically important Fort Duquesne. The fighting became part of a wider conflict between the

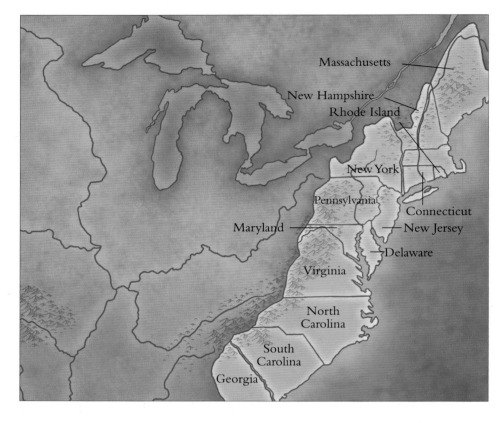

Below: George Washington and his followers raise the British flag at Fort Duquesne in 1758.

European powers – the Seven Years War (1756–1763) – which would end with French defeat, leaving the British as the dominant European power on the continent of North America.

During the struggle the Native American tribes, then the most numerous group living in the American

Above: In 1775, 13 of the British colonies that had been established in the New World rebelled against British rule.

interior, maintained a series of shifting alliances with France and Britain in the hope of postponing what would soon become inevitable: their displacement by the European settlers who were flocking to the New World. When, in 1758, the British took control of the upper Ohio valley for the first time, with Washington once again involved in the campaign that culminated in the capture of Fort Duquesne, the tribes in the region switched their allegiance to the winners. By the end of 1760 France's influence was waning and it had surrendered Quebec, Montreal and Detroit. Fighting ended with the signing of the Treaty of Paris (1763). France ceded New Orleans and the Louisiana Territory west of the Mississippi River to Spain and the rest of its mainland North American territories to Britain.

THE COST OF WAR

The cost of fighting the Seven Years War in both Europe and America had more than doubled the British national debt. Britain argued that its American colonies had benefited from the war, since they were no longer threatened by France's imperial ambitions in the New World, and they should now show their gratitude for their greater sense of security by accepting a number of new taxes imposed on them to help ease the burden of Empire. The Americans naturally disagreed. Repeated attempts by Britain to increase revenue from its colonies in the decade following the signing of the Treaty of Paris created a widening political chasm.

In 1765, the British parliament approved the Stamp Act, which put a tax on any printed paper used in the American colonies, including legal documents, contracts, newspapers and playing cards. The revenue raised in this way was to pay for the expense of maintaining British troops in the colonies. The act was passed without consultation with the colonists.

Below: Paul Revere, an express rider, alerted the people of Lexington to the imminent arrival of regular army troops.

In Massachusetts, John Adams, a lawyer who would become the second president of the United States, was drawn to the radical cause. Prompted by his opposition to the Stamp Act, he first entered the public arena in 1765, arguing that such taxes should be agreed to by those who would pay them, and not simply imposed: this had been a constitutional principle since the signing of Magna Carta, but was now being denied to colonists, though they were still British subjects. The Stamp Act proved unenforceable. It was repealed in 1766, though not before it had provoked the memorable slogan of independence: "No taxation without representation." Adams would become one of the leading advocates of American independence as resentment against Britain grew in the colonies.

QUARTERING ACT

In the same year that the Stamp Act was passed, the Quartering Act was extended from Boston throughout the colonies. It allowed for British troops to be billeted and provisioned in private homes without charge. Most colonies had accepted such terms in war, but in peacetime it was an imposition many Americans found unacceptable.

THE STAMP ACT

The attempt to impose the Stamp Act stirred political unrest throughout Britain's North American colonies. Those who would lead the call for American independence in influential colonies like Massachusetts and Virginia campaigned for its repeal. Patrick Henry, a prominent member of the House of Burgesses in Virginia, responded to the Stamp Act by issuing the Virginia Resolves, to assert their opposition to the tax. In response, the British-appointed governor of the state dissolved the legislature – an early sign of the more serious political confrontations to come between Britain and its American colonies.

Below: Patrick Henry delivering his most famous speech – "Give me liberty or give me death" – in 1775.

IMPORT DUTIES

Two years later, the Townshend Acts attempted to finance colonial administration through the imposition of taxes on a range of goods imported to America, including glass, paint, oil, lead and tea. In retaliation, Americans refused to order supplies from Britain and transatlantic trade suffered.

The relationship between Britain and its North American colonies continued to deteriorate, and it was the event of

MINUTEMEN

The Minutemen were volunteer rapid response units of the Massachusetts militia, formed during the 17th century to act as the first line of defence when emergencies arose. Although they lacked a centralized command, they were typically well trained and organized, selected from the younger, fitter members of the militia.

Left: A Minuteman, so named because these troops were ready to act at a minute's notice.

Rome might seek to claim it. They now saw the religious toleration for Catholics in Canada incorporated in the Quebec Act as a cynical manoeuvre intended to keep what Americans regarded as 'the fourteenth colony' loyal to the Crown. Some argued that this was an attempt to undermine the Protestant faith in North America.

The Quebec Act achieved its desired result: Canada would remain loyal to Britain, despite the American colonists' later attempt to capture Quebec. It would also become a sanctuary for American Loyalists, who fought for the Crown against the Patriots in what would be a civil war as well as a struggle for colonial independence.

Massachusetts became the front line in the confrontation between the colonies and Britain. The British forces, massed in Boston, were targets for American hostility as New England prepared for war. On 18 April 1775, Paul Revere, a New England silversmith who supported the call for rebellion, rode into American history when he travelled from his home in Boston to Lexington to warn the local militia that the British were on their way to search and destroy military supplies being hoarded by the colonists. Forewarned, the Massachusetts Minutemen confronted the British troops at Lexington and Concord, in the opening battles of the American War of Independence.

1773 known as the Boston Tea Party that came to symbolize the extent of American discontent. In its aftermath, the British government closed the harbour in March 1774 and in May Parliament approved the Coercive Acts, aimed at punishing Massachusetts. These additional measures tightened British control over the colony and effectively suspended its governmental charter, the origins of which could be traced back to the establishment of the Puritan colony in Massachusetts Bay in 1630.

THE CANADIAN COLONIES

Meanwhile, with increasing unrest in the south, the British government tried to secure the allegiance of the French Canadians, who were the overwhelming majority of those living in Quebec. The Quebec Act, passed in December 1774, reformed the governance of the area and added to the displeasure of New England colonists. Many of them were descended from those Puritans who had come to the New World to counter the prospect that the Church of

THE BOSTON TEA PARTY

The British East India Company monopolized the tea trade between India and the colonies, but the high tax levied on the product encouraged Americans to boycott it and buy cheaper tea smuggled from Holland, which affected the company's profitability. In May 1773 the Tea Act was passed, permitting the company to sell directly to the colonies free of British duty, undercutting American wholesalers. For the colonists it was another example of arbitrary rule. In protest, in December 1773 men disguised as Native Americans boarded ships moored in Boston harbour and unceremoniously dumped the tea they carried overboard. The act of defiance dramatized the colonists' increasing hostility to British policies and rallied support for the patriot cause. John Adams, the future president, confided in his journal: "This destruction of the tea is so bold, so daring, so intrepid and so inflexible, and it must have so important consequences and so lasting that I can't but consider it an epoch in history."

Below: The Boston Tea Party was an act of rebellion that shocked the English king.

WASHINGTON TAKES COMMAND
1775

In December 1758 George Washington had resigned from the Virginia regiment. He had sought a commission in the British Army, but this had been refused. Although he was the regiment's commanding officer his military reputation counted for nothing: British officers in North America, who had gained preferment through royal patronage rather than by merit, were contemptuous of the colonial militia, and indeed regarded most Americans as little more civilized than the Native Americans with whom they shared the continent. So he abandoned his military career and in January 1759 married the widow Martha Custis. Her wealth helped him to enter Virginia's colonial aristocracy and develop his estate at Mount Vernon, but he soon found that his prospects were tied into an imperial system that controlled the market price of tobacco, his principal source of income, upon which he relied to sustain the expensive lifestyle his social position demanded. Washington, like many Virginia planters – Thomas Jefferson was another – became consistently and chronically indebted to his London mercantile house.

In 1763, with the war with France over, a royal proclamation made the Ohio Territory part of an extensive Indian reservation. Further colonial settlement was banned. For Washington, who himself had interests in land there and who considered America's westward expansion inevitable, it symbolized yet more unwarranted British interference in the future of North America.

Resenting his British military superiors, his financial dependence on London merchants and his suspicions that the king would ultimately grant land rights in the interior to British rather than Virginian aristocrats gave Washington good reasons to support the cause of independence as it became the major issue in mid-18th century American politics. For more than a decade, in common with others in the colonies his resentment against British rule grew.

THE CONTINENTAL CONGRESS
In 1773, Benjamin Franklin, one of the most famous Americans of the day, suggested that all the colonies should meet to discuss their grievances against the British. Initially there was little support for the idea, but in September 1774 twelve colonies (Georgia stayed away) sent representatives to the first Continental Congress. Washington was among them. Meeting in Philadelphia,

Below: The Continental Congress was funded and directed by the Thirteen Colonies, and unified them for the first time under a provisional representative government.

the Congress agreed to rally support for a boycott of British goods. It also composed the Declaration of Rights and Grievances, addressed to King George III.

Early the following year, the British parliament passed an act restricting New England's trade to that with Britain alone. Determined to back its legislation with force, it met with equally defiant resistance from Americans.

At its second meeting in May 1775, with Georgia this time represented – the Continental Congress would create the Continental Army with George Washington in command. While he may not have anticipated the full magnitude of the task before him, he was at least prepared for the challenge. When he had journeyed from Virginia to Pennsylvania to attend the Congress he had packed his military uniform.

THE THIRTEEN COLONIES

British settlers had begun to establish colonies in eastern North America in the late 16th century, and by 1763 there were 20 British colonies on American territory north of Mexico. Thirteen united to fight against British rule and formed the original United States. Of the loyalist colonies, the five in the north would later form the Dominion of Canada, and East and West Florida in the south would be ceded by the British to Spain in 1783.

VIRGINIA

First colonial settlement: 1607
Colonial history: Jamestown established by the London Company.
Total population in 1790 census: 747,550
Total number of slaves in 1790 census: 292,627
Electoral College votes in 1789: 12 (2 votes not cast)

NEW JERSEY

First colonial settlement: 1618
Colonial history: Dutch settlement; British control (1664).
Total population in 1790 census: 184,139
Total number of slaves in 1790 census: 11,423
Electoral College votes in 1789: 6

MASSACHUSETTS

First colonial settlement: 1620
Colonial history: Plymouth Colony (1620); Massachusetts Bay Colony (1630). Colony united (1691), annexing Maine.
Total population in 1790 census: 378,556
Total number of slaves in 1790 census: 0
Electoral College votes in 1789: 10

NEW HAMPSHIRE

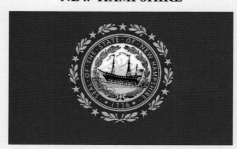

First colonial settlement: 1622
Colonial history: Originally part of Maine; separate colony (1629), annexed by Massachusetts (1641–3). Separate colony 1679 onwards.
Total population in 1790 census: 141,899
Total number of slaves in 1790 census: 157
Electoral College votes in 1789: 5

PENNSYLVANIA

First colonial settlement: 1623
Colonial history: Settled by Dutch and Swedes; British control (1664), granted to William Penn (1681).
Total population in 1790 census: 433,611
Total number of slaves in 1790 census: 3,707
Electoral College votes in 1789: 10

NEW YORK

First colonial settlement: 1624
Colonial history: New Netherland; British control (1664): renamed New York.
Total population in 1790 census: 340,241
Total number of slaves in 1790 census: 21,193
Electoral College votes in 1789: 8 (none appointed in time for election)

MARYLAND

First colonial settlement: 1634
Colonial history: Charter granted by King Charles I to Cecil Calvert.
Total population in 1790 census: 747,550
Total number of slaves in 1790 census: 292,627
Electoral College votes in 1789: 12 (2 votes not cast)

CONNECTICUT

First colonial settlement: 1635
Colonial history: Settled from Massachusetts and other colonies.
Total population in 1790 census: 237,648
Total number of slaves in 1790 census: 2,648
Electoral College votes in 1789: 7

RHODE ISLAND

First colonial settlement: 1636
Colonial history: Settled from Massachusetts; given royal charter (1663).
Total population in 1790 census: 69,112
Total number of slaves in 1790 census: 958
Electoral College votes in 1789: Constitution not ratified in time for the election

DELAWARE

First colonial settlement: 1638
Colonial history: Settled by Swedes; Dutch control (1655); British control (1664).
Total population in 1790 census: 59,096
Total number of slaves in 1790 census: 8,887
Electoral College votes in 1789: 3

NORTH CAROLINA

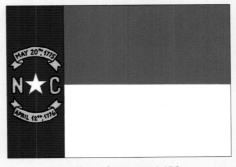

First colonial settlement: 1653
Colonial history: Carolina settled from other colonies; separated from Virginia: land granted to private company (1663).
Total population in 1790 census: 395,005
Total number of slaves in 1790 census: 100,783
Electoral College votes in 1789: Constitution not ratified in time for the election

SOUTH CAROLINA

First colonial settlement: 1670
Colonial history: Separated from North Carolina (1712) with appointment of separate governor; became crown colony (1729).
Total population in 1790 census: 249,073
Total number of slaves in 1790 census: 100,783
Electoral College votes in 1789: 7

GEORGIA

First colonial settlement: 1733
Colonial history: Private company granted land by King George II of England.
Total population in 1790 census: 82,548
Total number of slaves in 1790 census: 29,264
Electoral College votes in 1789: 5

THE FLAG OF THE UNITED COLONIES

Above: The Betsy Ross flag dating from 1777 shows 13 stars, each representing a colony, on a blue background. The 13 red and white stripes also each represent a colony. The stars are arranged in a circle, symbolizing perpetuity, and together they represent a new constellation. Five-pointed stars were revolutionary in flag design.

Above: The Francis Hopkinson flag (1777) shows the 13 stars staggered in alternate rows. Both flags were in use at the same time.

THE WAR OF INDEPENDENCE

1775–1782

John Adams, one of the founding fathers and a driving force in the battle for independence, like Washington, attended the first two meetings of the Continental Congress, and he later took credit for nominating Washington to command the Continental army. Whereas the colonel from Virginia was the unanimous choice for leader, in the confused atmosphere of the time there was still a debate over the need to raise a Continental army, rather than relying on separate forces from each colony to confront the British on American soil. When that issue was resolved, Washington accepted the commission.

Now a rebel fighting against the British Crown, Washington faced his greatest political, personal and military challenge. The odds on victory were long, but the consequences of defeat were profound. Even if he survived the war, on the losing side, he could be hanged as a traitor. Moreover, this was not yet a fight between nations. Thirteen colonies, each protective of their own interests and prone to rivalries among themselves, were taking on the world's most formidable military power.

Washington's war with the British began with the Siege of Boston and ended six years later with another siege at Yorktown, Virginia. After its surrender, the British army marched out of the town while their band played 'The World Turned Upside Down'. It had been. Despite losing more battles than he won during the long campaign, and although he did not believe it at the time, Washington had achieved America's independence. It was the persistence of the Patriots, coupled with the fact that their successes came at critical times in the conflict, and ultimately with the support of the French, that had earned them their victory.

VALLEY FORGE

In 1776, in New York, Washington confronted General William Howe, who commanded the greatest military force ever seen on the North American continent. Not surprisingly, the British forced the American troops to retreat into Pennsylvania. On Christmas night, however, Washington took the fight to the enemy. Crossing the Delaware River in the depths of the New England winter, he launched a successful surprise attack on the garrison at Trenton, which was manned by mercenaries recruited by the British from Hesse in Germany. This, together with his victory at Princeton just over a week later, revived what had been dangerously close to a lost cause.

During 1777, Washington lost important battles at Brandywine Creek and Germantown in Pennsylvania. In October, however, his generals, Horatio Gates and Benedict Arnold (later to become America's most notorious traitor) defeated the British General Burgoyne's forces at the Battle of Saratoga in New York.

The year ended with Washington moving his army into winter quarters at Valley Forge. It was a harsh winter. The general's stoicism as he, together with his troops, endured cold, disease, and a lack of food, symbolized American resolve in a war that Washington realized could be won through such heroic perseverance. It was at Valley Forge that Baron von Steuben, who had served in the Prussian army, made a vital contribution to America's war effort. He trained Washington's troops to such a professional standard that they were able to fight on equal terms with the British forces, now commanded by General Sir Henry Clinton, and the Americans avoided defeat during the Battle of Monmouth Court House in May 1778.

THE TIDE TURNS

On 10 July 1778 France declared war on Britain, exploiting its rival European power's problems in the New World. France's promised international aid was of little immediate help to America, as the French military contingent took time to arrive. For two more years

Left: The Battle of Lexington marked the start of the American revolution.

Right: More than seven years after fighting broke out, Washington returned to New York triumphant in 1783. He had secured independence for the colonists and would be the nation's first president.

Washington's army hung on in the north, suffering increasingly from lack of resources and eventually verging on collapse. Meanwhile the British waged a successful campaign against the southern colonies. When Clinton captured Charleston, South Carolina, in May 1780, it was America's worst defeat of the war. He then withdrew to his New York headquarters, leaving General Lord Charles Cornwallis in charge of British forces in the south.

The following year America's fortunes changed. Throughout the south, General Nathanael Greene used guerrilla tactics to harass the British, and in February 1781 another of Washington's generals, Daniel Morgan, inflicted a heavy defeat on Cornwallis's troops at Cowpens in South Carolina. In March the Americans won the Battle of Guilford Court House in North Carolina. With the British still threatening Virginia, Washington was now able to draw on French support and turned his attention from New York to his home state.

SURRENDER AT YORKTOWN

Cornwallis had moved his army to the Yorktown peninsula. Mistakenly believing that Clinton wanted him to remain there, instead of trying to break through the French and American lines, he stayed where he was. Meanwhile Washington and the French commander moved their combined forces south. On the way, Washington entertained his French ally at Mount Vernon, the first time he had seen his home in six years. On 15 September the American and French forces laid siege to the British

Right: Benjamin Franklin and Richard Oswald discussing the peace treaty between Britain and America in Paris.

army and on 19 October it was over. Cornwallis's surrender at Yorktown precipitated America's triumph.

The following year negotiations between the two sides began in Paris. The peace treaty was finally signed in September 1783. On 22 December Washington arrived in Annapolis, Maryland, to celebrate the victory. In a final heroic gesture, he resigned his commission. He was the most famous rebel in America.

THE DECLARATION OF INDEPENDENCE
1776

By 1776 American resentment against the British was becoming increasingly personal, with profound consequences. It focused on King George III and the institution from which he derived his power: the monarchy. In January, Thomas Paine published *Common Sense*, whose many readers included George Washington. Paine's arguments were persuasive: "But where … is the King of America? I'll tell you Friend, he reigns above, and doth not make havoc of mankind like the Royal Brute of Britain. Yet that we may not appear to be defective even in earthly honours,

let a day be solemnly set apart for proclaiming the charter … by which the world may know, that so far as we approve of monarchy, that in America THE LAW IS KING."

To become truly independent, the colonies would have to accept the need to reject not only British rule, but also the British system of government. John Adams and Thomas Jefferson (who became the second and third presidents) took the lead in moving the Continental Congress towards this radical vision. Adams drew up widely read guidelines for creating a republican

government and was largely responsible for the passage of a congressional resolution in May, encouraging the colonies to draft their own constitutions. At the same time Jefferson, also in Philadelphia to attend the Congress, was involved in discussions about a constitution for his home state. On 11 June, however, following the tabling of a resolution proposed by Virginia and seconded by Massachusetts: "That these United Colonies are, and of right ought to be, free and independent States", both men were distracted by a fresh task, that of presenting for Congress's approval America's Declaration of Independence.

THE DECLARATION

John Adams, who thought the more important job would be to advocate its adoption by Congress, left the writing of the declaration to Jefferson. A few days later, Jefferson had finished. He showed his work to Adams and to Benjamin Franklin, the author, inventor and statesman, and the most famous American of his time. They were the two colleagues whose opinions he most respected, and he accepted their minor amendments. He was less happy when Congress insisted on some major changes and revisions, which cut the Declaration of Independence to three-quarters of its original length, but on 4 July 1776, after Adams' articulate and impassioned speech in its favour – Jefferson called him "our Colossus on the floor" – the final version was agreed.

At the time, few realized that it was a decisive moment in American history. The cause of independence had been articulated in the language of revolution. It was Jefferson's concise and elegant expression of the philosophy of

Left: The Declaration of Independence was signed by congressmen from each of the Thirteen Colonies.

Left: King George III, whom Jefferson held to be personally responsible for the course of events that had led to America taking the irrevocable step of declaring its independence from Britain.

in shaping America's future. Like Adams, Jefferson believed that citizens should agree the form of government under which they lived, rather than be subjects of a monarch imposed on them by an accident of birth. The king had embroiled his nation and its American colonies in war. The desire to prevent such abuses of executive power would influence Americans – not least Jefferson's great political ally, James Madison – when they turned their attention to designing a constitution for a nation and to creating the office of president of the United States.

Below: Benjamin Franklin, John Adams and Thomas Jefferson drafting the Declaration of Independence.

natural rights and his vision of America's future as a democratic republic that meant that his words not only spoke to his contemporaries but would also become an inspiration for future generations: "We hold these truths to be self-evident, that all men are created equal, that they are endowed by their Creator with certain unalienable Rights, that among these are Life, Liberty and the pursuit of Happiness – That to secure these rights, Governments are instituted among Men, deriving their just powers from the consent of the governed – That whenever any Form of Government becomes destructive of these ends, it is the Right of the People to alter or to abolish it, and to institute new Government, laying its foundation on such principles and organizing its powers in such form, as to them shall seem most likely to effect their Safety and Happiness."

The remainder of the declaration, including Jefferson's long diatribe against George III, was also significant

THE FRAMING OF THE CONSTITUTION

1787

When James Madison (who would become the fourth president of the United States) joined Virginia's delegation to the Continental Congress in 1780, the war against the British king had yet to be won, but thanks to the arguments of Adams and Jefferson, monarchy was already only a memory for the Americans. As Francis Lightfoot Lee from Virginia, who had signed the Declaration of Independence, had observed in 1776: "Constitutions employ every pen."

With the Declaration, the colonies – now states – had become politically sovereign. They worked to 'institute new government' to replace the one they had rejected. More accurately, they created new governments, acting as if independent of each other as well as of Britain. The question remained as to the state of the nation: indeed, was there a nation at all?

THE ARTICLES OF CONFEDERATION

By 1777 the Continental Congress had drafted the Articles of Confederation. These allowed it to direct the war effort and to frame a co-ordinated foreign policy on behalf of all the colonies, but by the time Madison arrived in Philadelphia to represent Virginia in the Congress, not all states had ratified them. It was not until March 1781, a mere six months before Washington marched on Yorktown, that the last state (Maryland) agreed their terms.

Even though the Articles referred to "The United States of America", they committed the states only to "a firm league of friendship with each other for their common defense, the security of their liberties, and their mutual and general welfare". They envisaged a confederation of sovereign states, rather than the creation of a nation.

Each state had one vote in the representative Congress, and there was no mention of an executive office to provide political leadership. Having identified the monarch's abuse of power as the provocation for taking up arms, Americans remained suspicious of any constitutional and institutional arrangements that might lead to similar results once they had freed themselves of British control.

After the war, there was a similar suspicion of executive authority in the newly independent states. The state legislatures became the principal seats of political power, but their members were often elected annually, and control oscillated between competing factions. The result was political instability.

Below: George Washington was a natural choice to preside over the debate at the Constitutional Convention.

By the mid-1780s, there were some, like Madison, who worried that internal division between the states and political unrest within them would undermine not only the independence George Washington had fought for but also the revolutionary thinking about republican government that Adams and Jefferson had advocated.

Moreover, Washington, the former rebel, had now retired from public life, and the two revolutionaries were abroad: Jefferson had gone as American ambassador to France in 1784; Adams had remained in Europe after the Paris peace negotiations and was appointed ambassador to Britain the following year. When Jefferson visited Britain, he and Adams attended the court of George III, and the king made a point of publicly snubbing them: testament to the importance of their roles in achieving American independence. They were both still in Europe when Madison, the architect of the Constitution of the United States, arrived at the centre of the political stage in order to help preserve it.

In August 1786 Daniel Shays, who had fought at the battles of Bunker Hill and Saratoga, led a rebellion in Massachusetts of farmers who were suffering from debt as a result of the

state's high taxes. The following month, at a meeting in Maryland, Madison and Alexander Hamilton agreed the need for a Constitutional Convention that would seek to remedy the perceived deficiencies of the Articles of Confederation. A stronger national government might help the states avoid such political turbulence. It would, as Madison realized, "decide forever the fate of republican government".

Above: The Constitution, agreed in 1787, created the office of president of the United States.

THE CONSTITUTIONAL CONVENTION

Once again, Washington left Mount Vernon to travel to Philadelphia. In May 1787, as one of 55 representatives from the 13 states, he took his place as president of the Convention, which promptly ignored the task with which it had been charged – revising the Articles of Confederation. Instead it considered the Virginia Plan, proposed by Madison. This was a radical idea for a new national government.

For Madison, the opening words of the eventual document embodied its true political significance. "We the people" rather than "We the states" were the sovereign authority that instituted the government of the United States. This was again revolutionary. 'The people' – however that term was defined – would agree the powers of

Left: Independence Hall in Philadelphia, the meeting place of the first Continental Congress and a national landmark.

the United States government rather than, as had been the case, have the states define what it might do. The federal government could act independently, although it would preserve a political relationship with the states, the exact nature of which would become a matter of continuous negotiation.

It followed that, like the states themselves, the United States needed a set of institutions that would allow it to exercise its independence without abusing its power. Here Madison adhered to the conventional wisdom that had been best summarized by John Adams in 1775: "A legislative, an executive and a judicial power comprehend the whole of what is meant and understood by government. It is by balancing each of these powers against the other two, that the efforts in human nature towards tyranny can alone be checked and restrained."

This was what the Constitution tried to achieve. In a series of political compromises, the Convention created "separated institutions sharing powers"

Above: The Constitution was signed on 17 September 1787. Two years later, George Washington became America's first president.

within a federal system in which both the people and the states had a political stake. The first article set up the Congress. The popularly elected House of Representatives, initially with 65 members, and the Senate, in which each state had two senators chosen by their legislatures, had to agree what could become law. The third article provided for a Supreme Court in which judicial power was invested.

Article two, though, was just as significant for the nation's future. It stated that "the executive Power shall be invested in a President of the United States of America" who would hold office for a term of four years.

THE FEDERALIST PAPERS
In September 1787, as the Convention finished its work, Benjamin Franklin was asked what it had achieved.

FEDERALISTS AND ANTI-FEDERALISTS
As they fought the battle for its ratification, supporters and opponents of the Constitution that had been agreed at the Philadelphia Convention identified themselves as Federalists or Anti-Federalists (those who supported ratification of the Constitution and those who did not). One important intervention in the argument by the Federalists came when Alexander Hamilton, James Madison and John Jay collaborated in writing the Federalist Papers to persuade doubters of the merits of the plan for a national government. In the end the Anti-Federalists obtained a significant concession: in order to achieve ratification of the Constitution, the Federalists accepted the Anti-Federalist argument that a Bill of Rights should be added to the document in order to guarantee that essential individual freedoms were preserved.

His answer was simple: "A Republic, if you can keep it." A more fundamental question was whether the states would accept the new Constitution and the powerful federal government that Madison and his allies had proposed. It would come into effect once nine of the 13 states had ratified it, but reality dictated that if important states – among them New York – rejected it, the design for a national government would be in tatters. The Federalist Papers, written by Madison with Alexander Hamilton and John Jay, aimed to persuade the people of New York to accept the plan. As future generations tried to interpret the language of the Constitution, this collection of essays became important in explaining what those who framed the Constitution had in mind, the problems they faced and the ways in which they thought they had overcome them.

In July 1788, New York was the eleventh state to ratify the Constitution. It was eventually agreed unanimously,

but not before the Anti-Federalists had argued for the addition of a Bill of Rights. This, again designed mainly by Madison, was incorporated as the first ten amendments to the Constitution. Agreed in 1791, it established a stockade of individual rights, including freedom of speech and religion, into which government should not be allowed to enter.

THE OFFICE OF PRESIDENT

Despite their distrust of executive power, those discussing the office of president in Philadelphia were not too prescriptive as to its form. They accepted that the president should have a role both as a politician (with a limited veto on congressional legislation) and as head of state. The chief executive was designated commander-in-chief of the nation's armed forces, but was given few specific powers: principally those of pardon, treaty-making and appointment – notably of Supreme Court justices. The president was also required to keep

the Congress informed "of the State of the Union" and to "recommend to their consideration such measures" as were judged "necessary and expedient". In cases where the president might be charged with "Treason, Bribery or other high Crimes and Misdemeanors" there was the sanction of impeachment and removal from office.

The Convention made progress because it had a candidate in mind. George Washington was once again to be trusted with a critical role that would shape America's future. But there was to be no coronation. In keeping with the principles of a democratic republic, the presidency was open only to those who offered themselves for election to it.

Below: The construction of the Capitol building, the home of Congress and seat of government, began soon after the Constitution was ratified. President Washington laid the cornerstone of the building in September 1793.

THE ELECTORAL COLLEGE
CHOOSING THE PRESIDENT

According to James Madison's notes of the proceedings, when, on 4 September 1787, the Constitutional Convention meeting in Philadelphia discussed how the president should be selected, James Wilson of Pennsylvania confessed that he thought the matter to be "in truth the most difficult of all on which we have had to decide".

Of the many ideas that were considered, three that were rejected pointed the way to the political compromise that was eventually reached. First, the president was not to be selected by the federal Congress: it made the office dependent on the legislature, and thus compromised the essential principle of a separation of powers. Second, the state legislatures were not to choose between candidates because this would upset the delicate balance between state and federal power that was the basis of the principle of federalism. Finally, direct election was opposed, not only because it gave too much influence to the most populous states – who by merely voting for their own candidates would be able to outnumber the voters of small states, whose interests would therefore not be reflected in the outcome – but also owing to a distrust of democracy and the electorate's capacity to make such an important decision.

The matter was decided on 8 September, when the electoral college came into being, though the term itself was not used in the Constitution. The electoral college became perhaps the least understood institution, but in political terms it was the most significant factor in shaping both the character of presidential campaigns and the outcome of presidential elections.

VOTING PROCEDURE
The Constitution outlined the workings of the college. Each state was to be allocated a number of electors equal to the number of representatives it had in the federal Congress (though the representatives themselves were barred from appointment as electors). The electors would then meet in their respective states. Each would have two votes and would cast these for their two favoured candidates. When all the votes from the states were counted, the person who topped the ballot would become president and the runner-up would become vice president.

There was one other requirement. If it happened that no candidate gained an outright majority of electoral college votes, then the federal House of Representatives would determine who was to become president, choosing from among the five nominees who had received the most support. In this event, each state delegation in the House would have one vote to decide the outcome of the election.

The electoral college system was complicated, and in practice it did not work in quite the way that had been intended at the outset. The idea was that each state would select members of the community who could be trusted with the responsibility to decide who would be the best candidate to serve as the nation's president. Initially, it was the state legislatures that determined who became a member of the electoral college. Gradually, however, the institution was given an injection of democracy, and the electors began to be chosen by popular vote in each state.

THE PRESIDENTIAL TICKET
Sometimes the elections of college members were held in districts, but as political parties developed and electors were pledged to vote for particular party nominees, the result was that a state's electoral college votes could be divided among candidates. Large states therefore moved towards a 'general ticket' electoral system. This meant that the winner of the state's popular vote gained all that state's electoral college votes. The smaller states followed this lead, not wishing to diminish what little influence they had over the outcome.

The principle of federalism was preserved as the states became the focus

Left: George Washington taking the oath of office on 30 April, 1789. His inaugural address established an important precedent.

FOR PRESIDENT   FOR VICE PRESIDENT

WM. McKINLEY.   THEO. ROOSEVELT.

of presidential elections. Candidates now had to put together a winning coalition of states in the electoral college. Depending on the patterns of political support, however, the system meant that it was possible for the candidate with the most popular votes not to gain a majority in the electoral college, and for the president to be elected without winning most people's support.

In the presidential election of 1800, another problem arose. The newly formed political parties were orchestrating matters – but one did not do so well enough. Thomas Jefferson and Aaron Burr, who were running as president and vice president respectively, each received the same number of electoral college votes. Under the election rules, it was the House of Representatives that eventually decided that Jefferson would become president. Once that matter had been resolved, a

Constitutional Amendment was agreed that separated the election of president and vice president to ensure that the situation could not happen again.

In the 1824 presidential election, no candidate gained an outright majority in the electoral college. Congress exercised its constitutional powers to place John Quincy Adams in the White House. The electoral college 'misfired' again in 1876, when, amid allegations of fraud and corruption, an Electoral Commission awarded disputed electoral college votes to Rutherford B. Hayes, who became president despite the fact that his opponent, Samuel J. Tilden, had won the popular vote.

More recently still, in 2000, the Supreme Court intervened to decide the result of the election, because George W. Bush and Al Gore contested the legality of votes cast in Florida, which were critical to the outcome of

Above: Presidential and vice-presidential nominees run on the same ticket and are chosen to appeal to different voters.

the contest. There have also been over 150 instances of 'faithless electors' – individual electors who for some reason have failed to vote for their party's designated candidate.

When such controversies occur, voices are raised in favour of reform. More usually, however, Americans seem still to be persuaded by Alexander Hamilton's view, writing in *Federalist 68*: "If the manner of it be not perfect, it is at least excellent. It unites in an eminent degree all the advantages, the union of which was to be wished for." That remains the hope, and indeed appeared to be the case when, on 4 February 1789, the electoral college met for the first time and unanimously elected George Washington as president.

GEORGE WASHINGTON

1789–1797

George Washington's family came from Essex, England. John Washington, his great-grandfather, was a clergyman, but was asked to resign when his fondness for alcohol affected his ability to spread God's word. He decided to start a new life in the New World, and settled in Virginia in 1657. He soon acquired a different reputation among the local Native Americans, who called him 'town-taker' after he exploited legal technicalities to deprive them of their land. In contrast, his most famous descendant, George Washington, born on 22 February 1732, would be regarded as a paragon of integrity. Nevertheless, Washington inherited some family traits, including his physical presence and height and an abiding interest in the ownership of land.

Washington was 11 years old when his father died. His half-brother, Lawrence, his elder by 14 years, looked after him through his adolescence, but at the age of 34, after a trip to Barbados hoping to cure his tuberculosis (during

Below: George Washington being sworn in as commander-in-chief of the newly formed American army in 1775.

WASHINGTON'S CABINET

During his first term in office, George Washington devolved responsibility for important areas of the new administration's activity to his principal advisors, who became members of his Cabinet. The key positions, established in 1789, were secretary of state, secretary of the treasury, secretary of war and attorney general. As the range of executive and federal government activity grew, other portfolios were added, but the president still had the final say in any major policy decisions that had to be made.

which Washington, who accompanied him, contracted smallpox), Lawrence succumbed to the disease. Mount Vernon, Lawrence's 1,000ha (2,500 acre) plantation, became part of George Washington's inheritance.

Washington did not have a college education. After his initial military career, his marriage to the wealthy widow, Martha Dandridge Custis, brought with it a family when he became stepfather to her two children,

Jack and Martha. He had no children of his own. Washington's involvement with politics began when he entered the Virginia House of Burgesses in 1759, the year after he had resigned his commission in the militia. His military experience led to the Continental Congress appointing him to command the American army during the War of Independence and his political stature was confirmed when he returned to public life to chair the Constitutional Convention in 1787.

While often maintaining a pose of indifference towards politics, Washington cultivated his reputation and disguised his ambition with displays of reticence. It was his military contribution to the cause of independence, the political legitimacy his presence gave to the Constitutional Convention, and the trust that his contemporaries placed in him that led to him being chosen, inevitably, as the nation's first president.

Born: 22 February 1732, Westmoreland County, Virginia
Parents: Augustine (1693?–1743) and Mary (1708?–89)
Family background: Farming
Education: Not formally educated
Religion: Episcopalian
Occupation: Soldier, plantation owner
Slave owner: Yes (in his will he freed his slaves)
Political career: Virginia House of Burgesses, 1759–74
Continental Congress, 1774–5
Chairman, Constitutional Convention, 1787–8
Presidential annual salary: $25,000 (Washington refused payment)
Political party: Federalist
Died: 14 December 1799, Mount Vernon, Virginia

Right: George Washington was the natural choice as first president of the newly formed United States of America.

PRESIDENT WASHINGTON

Washington took office on 30 April 1789, delivering his inaugural address in New York. Washington was initially both cautious and judicious in his approach to the use of executive power in a government that was still regarded with suspicion by many contemporaries. His first task was to define the shape of the office that he held. Everything he did established a precedent for the new republic. As he observed: "I walk on untrodden ground."

Washington's Cabinet, which, like its British counterpart, had no formal constitutional basis, was one in which politicians from Massachusetts, Virginia and New York held the key positions. John Adams was vice president. The first secretary of state – overseeing the new

THE VIRGINIA HOUSE OF BURGESSES

In 1619, the Virginia Company in London – concerned to attract more emigrants to the colony it had established in Jamestown, Virginia, in 1606 – agreed to devolve political power to an assembly. The governor, selected by the company, appointed a council of six members. Two representatives from each of the 11 plantations established there became members of the Virginia House of Burgesses, America's first elected legislature. As the colony grew, representation would be based on county divisions. The laws passed by the House were subject to the approval of the council, the governor and the company in London. Nevertheless it provided a forum for political discussion in which, 150 years later, prominent colonists such as George Washington, Patrick Henry and Thomas Jefferson would argue the case for American independence.

nation's foreign relations – was John Jay. He left to become the first chief justice of the Supreme Court, and was replaced by Thomas Jefferson. Alexander Hamilton from New York served as secretary of the treasury.

Reconciling such formidable political talents proved difficult. The major antagonism was between Hamilton and Jefferson and resulted from their fundamentally opposed visions of America's future: one in favour of a strong national government, and the other in favour of strong state government. Hamilton took advantage of the initial lack of political organization in Congress to create a coalition of like-minded supporters there. He was opposed by James Madison, now a member of the House of Representatives, who ensured the Jeffersonian persuasion also gathered support in the legislature. Two parties emerged: the Hamiltonian Federalists, in favour of strong central government,

and the Jeffersonian Republicans who saw the states as the nation's bedrock.

In Washington's first administration, the scale of the presidential office was small: he had more people working for him at his private estate at Mount Vernon than he employed to help him in New York. Early in his presidency he made visits to all the states then in the Union: in 1789 he went to New England, and then journeyed south the following year. His main duties were ceremonial, but he walked a political tightrope. Critics hinted that he was attempting to recreate the trappings of monarchy, and Washington had to be careful not to give the impression that King George III was about to be replaced by George I in America. He tried for as long as possible to maintain a role 'above politics', but as the partisan divisions emerged in the Cabinet and then in Congress, the president was forced to take sides.

MARTHA WASHINGTON

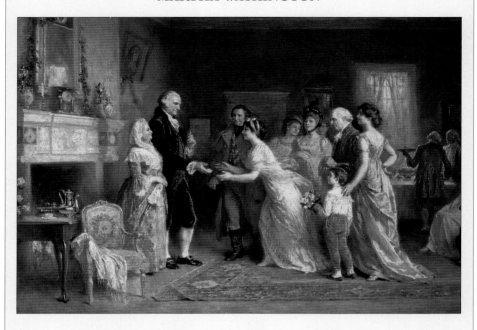

Martha Dandridge, 'Lady Washington', was born on 2 June 1731 in Virginia. Aged 19, she married Daniel Custis, who was 20 years her senior. He died in 1757, leaving her with two young children and a large tobacco-producing estate. It was there, two years later, in a mansion known as 'White House', that she married George Washington. During his presidency, she established a pattern of formal dinners and public receptions, attracting unfavourable criticism from those who thought their style too monarchical. Nevertheless, she remained

Above: The Washingtons entertained in style. Some accused them of thinking they were American royalty.

popular, especially among war veterans, who remembered her sharing their privations in winter quarters, notably at Valley Forge. For 40 years she supported her husband in Mount Vernon, on the battlefield, and in New York and Philadelphia while he was president. Before she died in 1802, she burnt their letters, preserving the privacy of her marriage for ever.

THE NATIONAL BANK
In 1791, Hamilton proposed the establishment of a national bank to hold deposits of federal funds, issue paper money, provide loans to the government and capital for investment. Congress passed the Bank Act that would set it up. Washington questioned whether or not he should veto this measure on the grounds that the Act was unconstitutional, and asked his secretary of state and his treasury secretary for their written opinions on the matter.

Jefferson based his argument on the Tenth Amendment, part of Madison's Bill of Rights agreed by Congress that

year, but yet to be ratified. He believed that "all powers not delegated to the United States, by the Constitution, nor prohibited by it to the States, are reserved to the States or to the people". For Hamilton, however, "if the measure … is not forbidden by any particular provision of the Constitution, it may safely be deemed to come within the compass of the national authority … A bank has a natural relation to the power of collecting taxes – to that of regulating trade – to that of providing for the common defense." Hamilton said Congress was right to approve the establishment of the National Bank.

Washington agreed, but the controversy was further evidence, if any was necessary, that his presidency was becoming increasingly involved in the political battles of the time.

POPULAR RE-ELECTION
In the 1792 presidential election, only six of the 15 states chose electors by popular vote. The qualification to take part in the election in those states varied widely: in the event, only 13,000 popular votes were cast. (According to the 1790 census, the United States had a total population of 3.9 million.)

Although Washington was identified more and more with the Hamiltonian Federalists, Jefferson recognized that his fellow Virginian still had the capacity to unite the nation. "North and South will hang together," he told the president, "if they have you to hang on." The electoral college vote confirmed this: again it

POLITICAL PARTIES
When Alexander Hamilton organized the Federalist party in support of his plans to create a strong central government, the opposition, led by Jefferson and Madison, called themselves Republicans. They sometimes accepted the label of Democrat-Republicans as a term of approval, in contrast to their opponents whom they characterized as aristocrats and quasi-monarchists. The Federalists used the same expression, Democrat-Republican, as a term of abuse, associating democracy with the excesses of mob rule in the French Revolution. After 1800, Jefferson's party dominated the political scene and the Federalist cause collapsed. During the 1820s and 1830s, as party competition re-emerged, Andrew Jackson's supporters appropriated the name of Democrat. Later on, the successors to their main opponents, the Whigs, once more became known as the Republican Party.

STATES ENTERING THE UNION DURING WASHINGTON'S PRESIDENCY:

VERMONT	KENTUCKY	TENNESSEE

VERMONT

Entered the Union: 4 March 1791

Pre-state history: Acquired by Britain (1763)

Total population in 1790 census: 85,341

Total number of slaves in 1790 census: 0

Electoral College votes in 1792 election: 3

KENTUCKY

Entered the Union: 1 June 1792

Pre-state history: Not a territory: the area was part of Virginia until achieving statehood

Total population in 1790 census: 73,677

Total number of slaves in 1790 census: 12,430

Electoral College votes in 1792: 4

TENNESSEE

Entered the Union: 1 June 1796

Pre-state history: Ceded by North Carolina to Federal government as Southwestern Territory (1789)

Total population in 1800 census: 105,602

Total number of slaves in 1800 census: 13,584

Electoral College votes in 1796: 3

---

was unanimous. Washington, unopposed in the election, reluctantly agreed to serve a second term.

Shortly after Washington had re-assumed office, in April 1793, war broke out between Britain and France, which was itself in the throes of revolution. Washington declared the United States' neutrality, keeping the nation out of the European conflict. However, the hostilities remained a threat to peace in the United States because Britain had maintained a military presence on American soil after the Treaty of Paris.

As tensions escalated, the president sent John Jay to London. His mission was to negotiate the removal of the British troops and put trade relations between Britain and the United States on a better basis. Jay succeeded in his first objective, but his American critics argued that he had been diplomatically out-manoeuvred by Britain, and had made a trade deal that was unfavourable to the United States. Jay's treaty, otherwise known as the Treaty of London of 1794, was passed by Congress only after the president had committed his considerable prestige to the battle.

FAREWELL ADDRESS

Washington left office at the end of his second term, establishing a final precedent that lasted 144 years. However, before stepping down, on 17 September 1796 he published his farewell address. In it he warned "in the most solemn manner against the baneful effects of the spirit of party" that had progressively impacted upon his administrations. He also advised the nation to "observe good faith and justice toward all nations. Cultivate peace and harmony with all … It is now our true policy to steer clear of permanent alliances with any portion of the foreign world." If his warning was ultimately in vain, his advice became a guiding principle for the nation's foreign policy for the next 150 years.

FINAL DAYS

Washington was 65 when he returned to Mount Vernon. His retirement was short, but one final act remained. He had become convinced that slavery, the South's 'peculiar institution', was morally wrong. If the principles of the Declaration of Independence were to

have any meaning, it had no place in a democratic republic; he felt that it threatened the nation he had helped to create. In 1798 he reportedly observed: "I can foresee that nothing but the rooting out of slavery can perpetuate the existence of our union."

His end came on 14 December 1799, but even in death, once again, he led by example. By a simple act, George Washington ensured that he added a lasting lustre to his military and political achievements. Ever mindful of his place in history, he made provision in his will for his own slaves to be freed.

Below: Mount Vernon, the ancestral home inherited by George Washington, and the house to which he retired.

ALEXANDER HAMILTON
FOUNDING FATHER

Alexander Hamilton has a unique place in American political history: he was a former secretary of the treasury and was killed in a duel by an incumbent vice president. It was one of the most famous duels recorded, and the final act in a controversial life, during which Hamilton made immense contributions to the causes of independence, revolution and the development of the United States of America.

John Adams called Hamilton "the bastard brat of a Scotch pedlar" which, although he may have intended it as libel, was an accurate description of Hamilton's origins. Born in 1755 on the Caribbean island of Nevis, he arrived in New York in 1772 and joined the Patriot cause. During the War of Independence, he served as Washington's aide-de-camp and at Yorktown he led an infantry charge against the British.

Below: Burr and Hamilton prepare to fight. Duelling was an established way of resolving matters of honour, although it was condemned by Washington and Franklin, and was being outlawed in some states.

In 1787 Hamilton issued the call for the Philadelphia Convention, which would agree the Constitution of the United States. There he outlined his vision of a national government, according to which the president and senators would hold office for life and Congress would have extensive influence in determining the laws of the land.

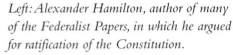

Left: Alexander Hamilton, author of many of the Federalist Papers, in which he argued for ratification of the Constitution.

This plan, radically different from Madison's idea of a federal republic, illustrated the competing philosophies that ultimately opened the political divide between them. Nevertheless, Hamilton accepted the compromises achieved in Philadelphia and collaborated with Madison in writing *The Federalist*, helping to persuade New York to ratify the Constitution.

COMPETING PARTIES

As secretary of the treasury in Washington's government, and a powerful influence in the Federalist party, Hamilton's main achievements, which were the financing of public credit and the federal government's assumption of the war debts of the states, were hardly calculated to seize the popular imagination. However, he realized that political independence and the future success of the United States depended upon its economic vitality. The Republicans accused him of favouring the industrial and commercial interests of the North over the agricultural concerns of the South. With Jefferson's election in 1800, Hamilton's influence and that of the Federalist party in national politics was largely eclipsed.

When Vice President Aaron Burr ran as an independent candidate in the 1804 race for governor of New York, Hamilton was his implacable opponent. His reported remarks at a dinner party were taken by Burr as a slight, sufficient to challenge Hamilton to a duel. Afterwards, Burr escaped to South Carolina despite being indicted for murder in two states: New Jersey, where their fatal meeting took place, and New York, where, on 12 July 1804, Hamilton had died from his wound.

JOHN ADAMS
1797–1801

Born: 30 October 1735, Braintree
(now Quincy), Massachusetts
Parents: John (1691–1761) and
Susanna (1709–97)
Family background: Farming
Education: Harvard College (1755)
Religion: Unitarian
Occupation: Lawyer
Slave owner: No
Political career: Continental
Congress, 1774–8
Commissioner to France, 1778
Minister to the Netherlands, 1780
Minister to England, 1785
Vice president, 1789–97
Presidential annual salary: $25,000
Political party: Federalist
Died: 4 July 1826, Braintree,
Massachusetts

John Adams's political misfortune was to become president after a widely respected and wildly popular incumbent had left office. He had served as Washington's vice president for eight years, and it was inevitable that he would remain in his shadow. As president, he faced some formidable challenges. Political divisions and party rivalries threatened domestic stability. France had interpreted Jay's treaty as creating a potentially hostile alliance between the United States and Britain and so there was also the prospect of war. Adams's major achievement was to preserve the peace, thereby ensuring that the nation survived a hazardous period of political turbulence.

LIFE BEFORE THE PRESIDENCY
Like George Washington and Thomas Jefferson, with both of whom his career was entwined, John Adams traced his

Right: John Adams, the first president to live in the newly completed White House.

family's roots in America back to the 17th century. He was the first president to graduate from Harvard, which was then a college rather than a university. His father had expected him to become a minister but, like many of his successors, he instead became first a lawyer, then a politician. He was not only a leading supporter of colonial independence but also an advocate of republican government and fiercely patriotic.

After serving in the first and second Continental Congress, and playing a critical role in the events leading to the Declaration of Independence, Adams spent time in France, Holland and

Britain before returning to America and becoming the first vice president of the United States. He disliked his eight years as Washington's understudy, moaning to his wife Abigail: "My country has in its wisdom contrived for me the most insignificant office that ever the invention of man contrived or his imagination conceived." Finally, in 1796, it was his turn to be president.

THE ELECTION OF 1796
His contemporaries recognized that Adams was irascible, cantankerous and argumentative, but since, like Washington, he had become identified

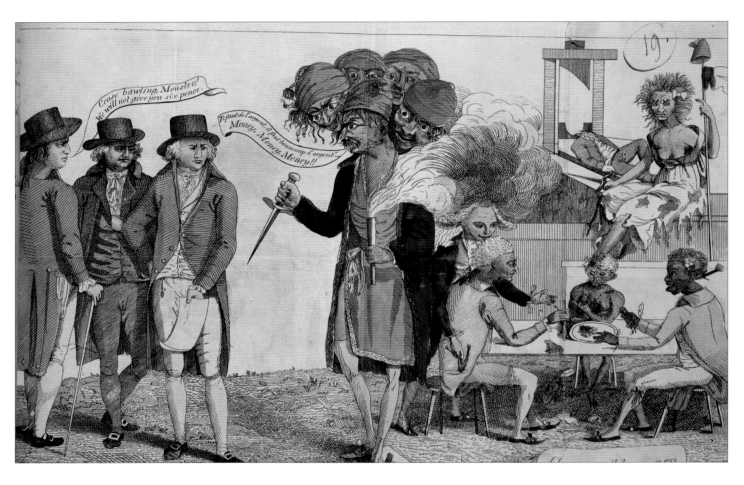

Above: A contemporary cartoon satirizes the French request for bribes before America's statesmen were received.

with the Federalist cause he was the party's preferred candidate. When the electoral college met in 1796, however, Alexander Hamilton tried to influence the southern states to support Thomas Pinckney from South Carolina instead of Adams, thinking he would be less independently minded. Hamilton's efforts misfired however, and merely led to the New England states refusing to vote for Pinckney. Thomas Jefferson, the Republican party's candidate, was the beneficiary: he gained only three fewer votes than Adams, beating Pinckney, and as a result Jefferson became vice president.

It fell to Adams, in his constitutional role as president of the Senate, to announce his own victory. He was inaugurated as president on 4 March 1797. Jefferson returned home: like Adams he placed loyalty to his political beliefs above the friendship that stretched back 20 years to the days when both men had argued for revolution.

ADAMS IN OFFICE

Adams's four years in office were dominated by the impact that the threat of war had on both domestic and foreign policy. In 1797 Adams sent three envoys to France in an attempt to secure peace. The outcome was the 'XYZ Affair', so called because these were the initials used for the three French agents who demanded a substantial bribe before any negotiations with the French foreign minister could take place. In 1798, when Adams made this public, it caused outrage in the United States.

ALIEN AND SEDITION ACTS

Rumours circulated of an imminent French invasion. In 1798, Federalists in Congress hastily passed four pieces of legislation, collectively called the Alien and Sedition Acts. The first lengthened the time before residents in the United States could apply for American citizenship. The second gave the president power to deport non-citizens – aliens – who were considered "dangerous to the peace and safety of the United States". The third permitted aliens whose loyalties were thought to lie with an enemy power, namely France, to be arrested and deported. The Sedition Act defined treason as including the publication of "false, scandalous and malicious writing" and was used to imprison editors of Republican newspapers.

In February 1799, Adams split the Federalist party and effectively destroyed his prospects for a second term when he announced he was making renewed diplomatic efforts to resolve the continuing 'quasi-war', which had involved American and French naval forces, by sending another delegation to France. A treaty was agreed, but Adams failed in his bid for re-election and the Federalists also lost control of the legislature. In 1802, the Republican-dominated Congress repealed the first of the Alien and Sedition Acts, which had aimed to deprive the party of its strong electoral following among recent arrivals from Europe. The remaining three acts had already been allowed to lapse when, during the two previous years, they had become due for renewal.

LIFE AFTER THE PRESIDENCY

Adams became the first incumbent president to be turned out of office. His defeat signalled the beginning of the end for the Federalist party, which never managed to win the presidency again. He retired to his farm in Quincy, Massachusetts. With his wife Abigail acting as go-between, he and Jefferson rehabilitated their relationship through a long and fascinating correspondence. If Adams's last words, "Thomas Jefferson survives", were a question, the answer was no: his friend had died in Virginia a few hours earlier on Independence Day, 1826.

Below: Adams Mansion in Quincy, the home of John and Abigail Adams.

ABIGAIL ADAMS

Abigail Smith, born in Massachusetts in 1744, married John Adams in 1764. Four of their children survived to adulthood (a fifth, a daughter, died aged two) and their son John Quincy Adams would later become president.

Although Abigail was separated from her husband for long periods, between 1784 and 1788 she joined him in France and Britain, returning to the United States when he became vice president. Her correspondence survives. She was unafraid of giving her husband forthright advice. While he took part in discussions leading to the Declaration of Independence she admonished him to "remember the ladies and be more generous and favourable to them than your ancestors. Do not put such unlimited power into the hands of the husbands." But he forgot and he did. She was a passionate Federalist; her critics complained she wielded too much influence, calling her 'Mrs President'.

Above: Abigail Adams is famed for her support of women's rights.

Following Adams's election defeat, the couple retired to Massachusetts, where she was instrumental in reviving his friendship with Thomas Jefferson. She died in 1818, three days after their 54th wedding anniversary.

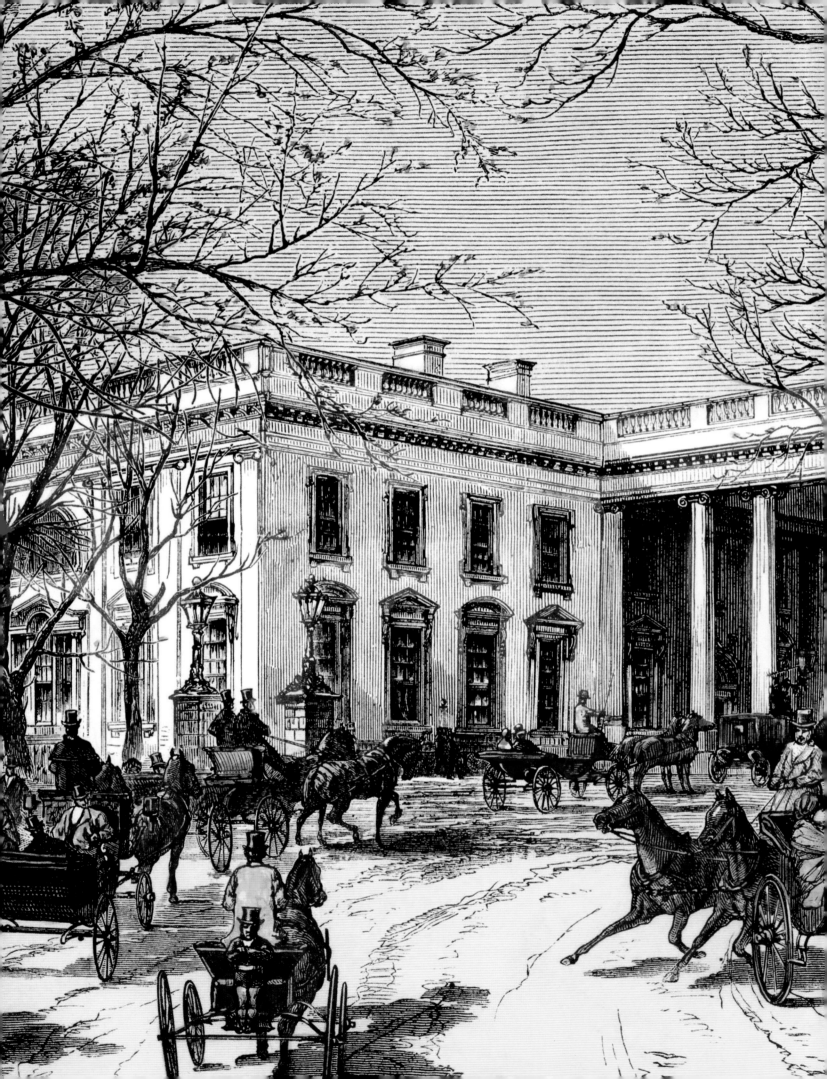

CHAPTER TWO

THOMAS JEFFERSON TO JAMES MONROE

1801–1825

THE 'VIRGINIA DYNASTY', PRESIDENTS JEFFERSON, MADISON AND MONROE, DOMINATED AMERICAN POLITICS IN THE EARLY YEARS OF THE 19TH CENTURY. EUROPEAN POWERS STILL HAD IMPERIAL AMBITIONS IN NORTH AMERICA, BUT IN NEGOTIATING THE LOUISIANA PURCHASE, JEFFERSON ENDED FRENCH TERRITORIAL INTEREST, AND MADE POSSIBLE THE UNITED STATES' MOVEMENT WESTWARD ACROSS THE CONTINENT. FOR HIS SUCCESSOR, THE THREAT FROM BRITAIN REMAINED AND IN 1812 MADISON WAS FORCED TO FIGHT WHAT WAS REGARDED AS A SECOND WAR OF INDEPENDENCE WITH THAT COUNTRY. INTERNATIONAL RELATIONS ALSO DOMINATED MONROE'S PRESIDENCY. HIS DOCTRINE, PROMULGATED IN 1823, WOULD DEFINE THE CONTOURS OF AMERICAN FOREIGN POLICY. THIS, THEN, WAS THE FORMIDABLE POLITICAL LEGACY OF THE 'VIRGINIA DYNASTY', FORMED IN THE CRUCIBLE OF A CRITICAL ERA IN THE DEVELOPMENT OF THE UNITED STATES OF AMERICA, 'THE FIRST NEW NATION'.

Left: The White House, the official presidential home, was completed in 1800.

THE PRESIDENTIAL ELECTION
1800

The presidential election of 1800 proved to be one of the most controversial in American history and was characterized by bitter personal attacks on members of both parties. It exposed a flaw in the Constitution's provisions for the election of the president and vice president, leading to the drafting of the Twelfth Amendment, which was ratified in 1804. It also marked the beginning of a period of Republican rule in government and the demise of the Federalist party.

There were four main candidates. John Adams, who was the incumbent president, and Charles Pinckney – the brother of Hamilton's favoured nominee four years earlier – represented the Federalists. The Republicans supported Thomas Jefferson and Aaron Burr.

The 16 states had 138 electors, so 70 votes were needed for a majority. The Philadelphia Convention had agreed that slaves should be counted as three-fifths of a free person in determining apportionment. This meant that in 1800, Jefferson had a potential advantage: Southern states had 12 more votes in the electoral college than they would have had if representation had been based on the free population alone. Jefferson, from Virginia, could expect to count on their support: indeed the South provided 53 of his electoral college votes. Nevertheless, the Republicans managed to make difficulties for themselves by failing to arrange for Jefferson to receive one more vote than Burr. This meant that there was no clear winner in the electoral college.

The Federalists were better organized. In the electoral college, they ensured that Pinckney was runner-up to Adams by allowing one elector to cast a solitary vote for someone else: John Jay, the governor of New York.

The dead heat between Jefferson and Burr meant that under the rules governing the electoral college, the contest would be decided by the House of Representatives. Before that happened, Jefferson made a crucial intervention that shaped the eventual outcome. It fell to him, as vice president and presiding officer of the Senate, to act as returning officer when the envelopes containing the electoral college votes were opened on 11 February 1801, and with this the problems began.

THE PROBLEM WITH GEORGIA
When Jefferson opened the envelopes it became apparent that Georgia had not complied with the statutory requirement to return two documents: one recording the names of the candidates for whom its four electoral votes had been cast and a second, signed by the governor, certifying the names of the electors selected by the state. Instead, there was a single piece of paper in Georgia's envelope. On one side it bore the governor's signed certificate and on the other the names of Jefferson and Burr with the signatures of the four electors underneath.

Had there been fraud? Had a second piece of paper been removed and the electors' votes scrawled on the back of the governor's document? Should the votes – four for the Republicans – be counted? Without Georgia, Jefferson and Burr (whose name on the ballot had guaranteed that the party won New York) had 69 votes each. Jefferson, as the Senate's returning officer, made a quick decision: Georgia's result was valid.

The acceptance of Georgia's votes meant that the Republicans had beaten

Left: Though Burr campaigned successfully for political positions he blamed his lack of prominence in that area on Hamilton.

Above: Charles Cotesworth Pinckney, from South Carolina, was the Federalist choice for vice president.

the Federalists. Their votes were still tied, however, and the winner from the Republican party still had to be decided. Had Georgia's votes been ruled out, no candidate would have achieved a majority in the electoral college, and the Federalist candidates, Adams, Pinckney and even John Jay would have remained in contention. As it was, the contest now was between Jefferson and Burr. The scene of political action moved from the Senate to the House of Representatives.

THE HOUSE DECIDES

In the House of Representatives, each of the 16 states had one vote, which was decided by ballot between the members for each state. The outcome would be decided on an absolute majority, so nine votes were needed to win. The Federalists had a majority in the House of Representatives, and they generally supported Burr in an attempt to prevent Jefferson becoming president. However, the Federalists' strength was concentrated heavily in the northern states of New England, enabling the

Right: After Jefferson and Burr received the same number of electoral college votes in the presidential election, the Twelfth Amendment (1804) separated the balloting for president and vice president.

Republicans to counteract it. They were able initially to influence six states' delegations in favour of Jefferson by a margin of a single vote. On the first ballot, therefore, the battle lines were drawn: Jefferson was preferred by eight states, Burr by six, and in two – Vermont and Maryland – the ballots were drawn and neither candidate was the winner.

Six days and 35 ballots later, after the votes had ebbed and flowed, and with supporters campaigning vigorously, Jefferson finally emerged victorious. James Bayard, a Federalist representative from Delaware, who in the final round of voting, along with his allies in Maryland and Vermont, cast blank ballots in order to break the impasse, wrote to Hamilton: "the means existed of electing Burr, but this required his co-operation. By deceiving one man (a great blockhead) and tempting two (not incorruptible) he might have secured a majority of the states." Hamilton's loathing for Burr had led him to work for Jefferson's election despite their mutual animosity.

To his critics, Burr was at fault for not indicating that he supported Jefferson's cause. It suggested that his personal ambition came before his loyalty to the Republican party. On the other hand, if he had aggressively pursued his self-interest, he might have split the Republicans and made the matter worse; instead his self-restraint helped towards the peaceful resolution of the election deadlock.

Before the crisis was over, it had threatened to escalate. A demonstration took place when a mob, suspicious that Federalists in the House were siding with Burr to prolong the constitutional confusion, gathered in the federal capital. The Republican governors of Virginia and Pennsylvania, James Monroe and Thomas McKean, called on their militias to prepare for action if it should prove necessary. The example of the French Revolution and its descent into violence and chaos was never far from their minds.

On 17 February 1801, the House decided. Through some political manoeuvring and a measure of luck, the American Republic had met and overcome a potentially disastrous challenge to its future. The author of its Declaration of Independence had triumphed in what he came to call "the Revolution of 1800": Thomas Jefferson was America's president elect.

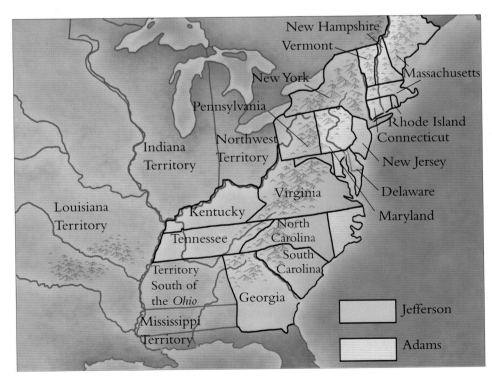

THE SUPREME COURT
THE HIGHEST COURT OF LAW

Convened for the first time in February 1790, the Supreme Court of the United States was the only court established by the Constitution. It was left to Congress to establish inferior courts, and to decide on the composition and procedures of all the courts.

The federal judiciary had been one of the most hotly debated issues during the framing of the Constitution, with Anti-Federalists seeing it as a means of tyrannizing the states, but for the first decade of its existence the judiciary was the weakest of the three branches of government: with no direction from the Constitution, the Supreme Court was unsure of its power over the laws passed by Congress. It had no permanent home and lacked prestige.

This situation changed at the beginning of the 19th century. In deciding a case that arose during the transition of power between retiring and incoming presidents, Chief Justice John Marshall, who had been appointed by John Adams, asserted the principle of judicial review, claiming for the Supreme Court the right to shape the law according to its interpretation of the Constitution. Its power to do so continues to rest on the precedent set by the case of Marbury v. Madison.

Above: John Marshall was instrumental in determining the judicial balance of power.

THE MARSHALL COURT

In January 1801, John Adams nominated John Marshall, then secretary of state, as the fourth chief justice of the Supreme Court. Marshall, born in 1755 in Virginia, was a contemporary of both Madison and Monroe, but he had gravitated to the Federalists rather than to the Republicans as those parties emerged in the early years of the republic. John Marshall and the future president Thomas Jefferson were distant cousins who disliked one another and who disagreed politically. The Senate confirmed Marshall's appointment just prior to its official count of the electoral college votes cast in the presidential election of the previous year.

In the febrile political atmosphere surrounding the outcome of the 1800 election, there was even a suggestion, possibly made by Marshall himself, that the chief justice should assume the presidency if there was no resolution to the political impasse that had resulted from the electoral college dead heat. In the end, however, he found ways of advancing his political views from his position on the Supreme Court. His tenure there of 34 years would far outlast the presidential administration of his cousin, to whom, in March 1801, he administered the oath of office.

MARBURY VERSUS MADISON

After the House of Representatives had finally voted Jefferson into the White House, and before he took office, President Adams made a concerted effort to appoint as many Federalist judges as possible – they became known as 'the midnight judges' – to ensure that the party would at least retain control of the courts under the administration of a Republican presidency.

Marshall combined his position as chief justice with his existing post as secretary of state and in that capacity he was responsible for ensuring that the newly appointed judges received the appropriate letters of commission. Those intended for 17 justices of the peace appointed by Adams remained undelivered by the time his administration ended, and at Jefferson's request Marshall's successor as secretary of state, James Madison, refused to send them on. The president's action was subject to

Left: The Supreme Court is the highest judicial body in the United States.

SUPREME COURT JUDGES

Originally there were six Supreme Court justices. In 1869 the number was fixed at nine. They are nominated by the president, and successive incumbents have tried to influence the Court's composition through their power of appointment, but their nominees must be confirmed by a majority vote in the Senate. They serve "during good behavior", in other words until they retire, die or are impeached, and the average tenure of Supreme Court justices is about 15 years. With its power of judicial review, the Court remains the heartbeat of American Constitutional government.

Below: The Supreme Court of 1911.

a legal challenge when one of the justices, William Marbury, petitioned the Supreme Court to force Madison to deliver the commissions, and the court was called upon to decide the case.

Marshall had set in motion events that would lead his court into a potential political minefield. If it insisted that Madison carry out his duty, which was seen to be its legal responsibility, then the administration would ignore it and its status within the framework of the federal government would be undermined. On the other hand, if the Supreme Court did not try to force the issue, it would look equally weak.

His solution to this dilemma was ingenious. Marshall reprimanded Jefferson for not ordering Madison to send William Marbury his commission. At the same time he argued that the provisions of the Judiciary Act of 1789, giving the Court the responsibility of judging the case, were unconstitutional. It was this aspect of Marbury v. Madison (1803) that had the greatest constitutional reverberations. Marshall effectively asserted that the Court alone should interpret the original intent of the written Constitution agreed in Philadelphia in 1787.

Since "the Constitution is superior to any ordinary act of the legislature; the Constitution, and not such ordinary act, must govern the case to which they both apply". Who makes that judgement? Marshall was in no doubt: "The judicial power of the United States is extended to all cases arising under the Constitution." In saying that the Supreme Court should interpret whether or not a law was constitutional, Marshall invested its justices with a political as well as a legal power to shape the contours of American politics.

As Jefferson pointed out, this principle of judicial review was potentially controversial: "The Constitution, on this hypothesis, is a mere thing of wax in the hands of the judiciary, which they may twist, and shape into any form they please." However, the full implications of Marshall's decision were not immediately felt. It was another 54 years before the Court again pronounced on a constitutional issue, and then, in the case of Dredd Scott v. Sandford (1857), it contributed to the deepening political crisis that was precipitating the nation towards the Civil War.

John Marshall remained chief justice until his death on 6 July 1835, having ensured that from Jefferson's time onwards no president could disregard either the constitutional force or the political impact of the decisions taken by the Supreme Court.

Below: The original meeting place of the Supreme Court in Old City Hall, Philadelphia, housed its six judges.

THOMAS JEFFERSON
1801–1809

Thomas Jefferson was 33 when he wrote the Declaration of Independence. He was born in 1743, in Shadwell, Virginia. His family, which on his father's side had Welsh ancestry, had settled in the state in the 17th century. He was a bright, committed student, graduating from William and Mary College, Virginia, in 1762.

Like John Adams, Jefferson practised law before becoming politically active. In 1768, he embarked on a lifetime project: building his mountain-top retreat at Monticello, Virginia. Four years later, Jefferson, like George Washington, married a wealthy widow: Martha Wayles Skelton. In 1782, following the birth of their sixth child, only three of whom survived beyond the age of two, Martha died. Jefferson remained a widower for the rest of his life.

Born: 13 April 1743, Shadwell, Virginia

Parents: Peter (1708–57) and Jane (1720–76)

Family background: Plantation owners, surveying

Education: William and Mary College (1762)

Religion: Not proclaimed

Occupation: Lawyer, planter

Slave owner: Yes

Political career: Virginia House of Burgesses, 1769–74

Continental Congress, 1775–6, 1783–5

Governor of Virginia, 1779–81

Minister to France, 1785–9

Secretary of state, 1790–3

Vice president, 1797–1801

Presidential annual salary: $25,000

Political party: Democrat-Republican

Died: 4 July 1826, Monticello, Virginia

A RISING POLITICAL STAR

In 1774 as a member of the Virginia House of Burgesses, Jefferson, overshadowed by the likes of George Washington and Patrick Henry, was not included in the state's delegation to the first Continental Congress. A year later he arrived in Philadelphia as the replacement for Peyton Randolph, his political mentor. His contemporaries saw his strength as lying not in his oratory but in the eloquence of his writing: when Adams left him to compose the Declaration of Independence, their judgement was vindicated.

Above: Thomas Jefferson's election represented the end of the Federalist party's influence in presidential politics.

As governor of Virginia during the War of Independence, Jefferson narrowly escaped capture by Cornwallis's cavalry. After his wife's death, he became ambassador to France, and was in Paris to witness the French Revolution. Following three years as Washington's secretary of state and four as Adams's vice president, as his party's acknowledged leader, and at the age of 57, he became president of the United States.

A POPULAR FIRST TERM

Jefferson's election was an important symbolic event: the Federalists abided by its controversial outcome and relinquished control of the executive. It also had another consequence.

In his inaugural address, Jefferson appeared to heed the advice that Washington had given when he warned of the threat that political parties posed to the republic. "But every difference of opinion is not a difference of principle. We have called by different names brethren of the same principle. We are all republicans – we are all federalists." This appeal to patriotic sentiment suggested that he would reach out across the partisan divide. That indeed was how relieved Federalists interpreted his words, giving them hope that there would be no political retribution following the increasingly acrimonious and polarizing debates that had taken place during the Adams administration. Jefferson's predecessor had left town rather than witness the inaugural ceremony of his successor.

However, the new president's strategy for ending party competition aimed to destroy the Federalists as a political force. Three weeks after his inaugural address he wrote: "Nothing shall be spared on my part to obliterate the traces of party and consolidate the nation." He hoped "to be able … to unite the names of federalists and republicans". In this he was largely successful. By the end of his first term, the Federalists were well on the way to becoming a spent political force.

The Republicans owed their continued electoral fortune in no small measure to the successes of Jefferson's first administration. In keeping with his philosophy of minimalist government, the president cut federal expenditure and the military budget, reduced the national debt, and abolished the tax on whiskey: all of which proved to be popular measures. At the same time, he pursued an aggressive policy towards the continuing harassment of American

Above: The Louisiana Purchase effectively doubled the territory held by the United States government.

merchant shipping in the Mediterranean. The US navy skirmished with Barbary pirates along the North African coast, winning enough of the time to fuel patriotic support for Jefferson's actions. However, the major political coup of his first term, which had enormous implications for the country's future, came in 1803.

THE LOUISIANA PURCHASE

When an impoverished Spain agreed that France could buy back Louisiana, giving Europe's great military power control of New Orleans (through which almost half of American exports then passed), and a base from which it might regain the American empire it had lost in the mid-18th century, Jefferson was naturally concerned. It was, he wrote, "the embryo of a tornado". He sent James Monroe to help Robert Livingston, America's representative in Paris, to negotiate the continued right to use New Orleans as a strategic port.

In April 1803, Napoleon Bonaparte, needing cash to finance his military campaigns in Europe, and stung by the loss of the force he had sent to the Caribbean to put down the slave revolt led by Toussaint L'Ouverture, decided

Below: In purchasing the Louisiana territory Jefferson acted independently of Congress, and set a precedent for increased presidential power.

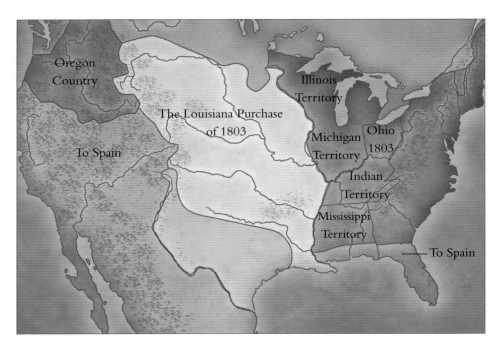

Above: The land gained by the Louisiana Purchase was organized into territories which then achieved statehood on their admission to the Union.

to liquidate his American assets. He offered to sell not only New Orleans, but also the rest of the Louisiana territory. This would effectively double the size of the United States. Jefferson had given Monroe a budget of ten million dollars to secure New Orleans. The price for the whole territory was fifteen million.

The opportunity was too good to miss, and Jefferson grabbed it, even though he admitted that: "The Executive, in seizing the fugitive occurrence which so much advances the good of their country, have done an act beyond the Constitution." The unique circumstances of the purchase, "a noble bargain" as the French foreign minister Talleyrand called it, allowed Jefferson to convince himself that in this instance pragmatic concerns about the

nation's security were more important than his constitutional principles. With a sense of the dramatic, he revealed that the purchase had been agreed on 4 July 1803. Five months later, Congress endorsed his action.

SECOND ADMINISTRATION

Jefferson won a convincing victory in the electoral college in 1804, beating Charles Pinckney by 162 votes to 14. There were now four times as many Republicans in the Senate as Federalists, and in the House of Representatives the margin was five to one. In his second inaugural address, the president congratulated the country on "the union of sentiment now manifested so generally" throughout the nation. Following the successes of his first four years, however, Jefferson's second term in the White House was something of an anti-climax.

The problem, once more, was Europe, and the effect upon the United States of the Napoleonic Wars. In his first inaugural address Jefferson had

SALLY HEMINGS

After Jefferson became president, his political opponents in the Federalist party circulated rumours that he was the father of several children by Sally Hemings, one of his slaves at Monticello (and the half sister of his wife). Historians speculated whether there was any truth in the accusation, and in 1998 scientists published DNA test results indicating that there was. The complexities of Southern attitudes to race and slavery were revealed in the character of one of the most eminent among the generation of Virginians who contributed to the founding and development of the United States.

Above: Julia Jefferson Westerinen, a descendant of Thomas Jefferson and his slave Sally Hemings.

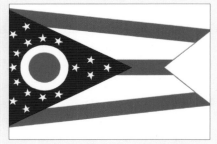

STATES ENTERING THE UNION DURING JEFFERSON'S PRESIDENCY: OHIO

Entered the Union: 1 March 1803
Pre-state history: Acquired by British (1763); ceded to US (1783); part of Northwest Territory (1787); first part of Territory to be organized for statehood
Total population in 1810 census: 230,760
Total number of slaves in 1810 census: 0
Electoral College votes in 1804: 3

MARTHA JEFFERSON

"My dear wife died this day at 11:45 A.M.," wrote Thomas Jefferson on 6 September 1782. Born in October 1748, Martha Wayles Skelton Jefferson was not quite 34 when she died. She had been a widow for four years when she married Jefferson on New Year's Day 1772, and her son by Bathurst Skelton, her first husband, had died, aged four, the previous year. She survived the birth of her sixth child by Jefferson by only a few months. Jefferson never remarried. He hosted White House events alone, occasionally calling upon Dolley Madison for help. His eldest daughter Martha 'Patsy' Randolph was his hostess in 1802 and again in 1806, when she gave birth to a son, named for James Madison, and the first child to be born in the White House.

Above: Martha Jefferson

Above: Dolley Madison

proclaimed that the United States would not involve itself in "entangling alliances" with other nations. Yet this did not mean that it could remain untroubled by events elsewhere. War between France and Britain in 1803 brought with it not only the opportunity of the Louisiana Purchase but also the huge costs associated with European naval blockades, which had a detrimental impact on America's transatlantic and Caribbean trade.

MISJUDGED MEASURES

Jefferson and James Madison, his secretary of state throughout his time in the White House, decided on measures that were politically inept and economically disastrous. Congress prohibited imports from Britain with the Non-Importation Act (1806) and followed it with the Embargo Act (1807), preventing US ships from leaving port. This proved so counter-productive that it was repealed in the year Jefferson left office. On his final day, he looked forward to retiring from public life: "Never did a prisoner, released from his chains, feel such relief as I shall on shaking off the shackles of power."

RETIREMENT

Jefferson lived out his remaining 17 years at Monticello, where the spiralling costs of his architectural project and his expensive tastes, including a liking for fine French wine, left him hopelessly in debt. He also supervised the construction of the University of Virginia in nearby Charlottesville.

Following Washington's example, and like John Adams, he was concerned with how history would judge him: his correspondence and renewed friendship with his predecessor allowed both to explain to each other and to posterity their political beliefs and principles.

With an immaculate sense of timing he died on 4 July 1826, aged 83. In his will he freed five members of the Hemings family, but not their mother, Sally. He gave instructions that his principal achievements should be engraved on his tombstone: "Author of the Declaration of Independence of the Statute of Virginia for Religious Freedom and Father of the University of Virginia". That he had been president was left unmentioned.

Below: Monticello, the mountain-top home that Jefferson spent his life building.

THE LEWIS–CLARK EXPEDITION
1803–1808

Even before negotiations had been concluded with Napoleon over the Louisiana Purchase, President Jefferson had proposed to investigate whether, by following the route of the Missouri and Columbia Rivers that flowed east and west of the Rocky Mountains, it was possible to journey across America to the Pacific Ocean. He was also motivated by scientific curiosity about the Pacific Northwest. On 28 February 1803, Congress approved the funds for an expedition. Jefferson selected Meriwether Lewis, a former army captain and neighbour from Virginia, whom he had taken to Washington as his private secretary, to lead the expedition. In turn, Lewis asked an old army friend, William Clark, to go with him as co-leader.

Jefferson took a personal interest in the preparations, sending Lewis to meet members of the American Philosophical Society, of which he was an active member (and its president from 1797 to 1815). At the Society's headquarters in Philadelphia, Lewis consulted with, among others, botanists, mathematicians and surveyors, receiving advice on the scientific instruments he should take with him to explore the West.

THE EXPEDITION

By the time Lewis and Clark reached their starting point near St Louis, in December 1803, the Louisiana Purchase had been made. They set out on 14 May 1804, making their way west up the Missouri River. Despite bad weather, navigational hazards, disciplinary problems and occasional harassment from Native Americans, by November they had reached what would later become the state of North Dakota. They stayed there for five months, in Fort Mandan, which they built and

Above: Meriwether Lewis and William Clark prepared for their expedition with the help of Native Americans.

named after a local Native American tribe. During that time they were joined by Toussaint Charbonneau, a French fur trader, and his wife Sacagawea, a Shoshone Indian. She would act as an interpreter, accompanying the expedition along with her newborn child, Jean-Baptiste. While they were at Fort Mandan, Lewis and Clark also sent back a number of items that they had collected to the president in Washington. Beside Native American artefacts, these included animal skins, examples of plants, soil and rocks, and even a live prairie dog.

In April 1805 the expedition moved on. Two months later, where the Missouri branched, they travelled south along the river until they came to a succession of waterfalls in what is now

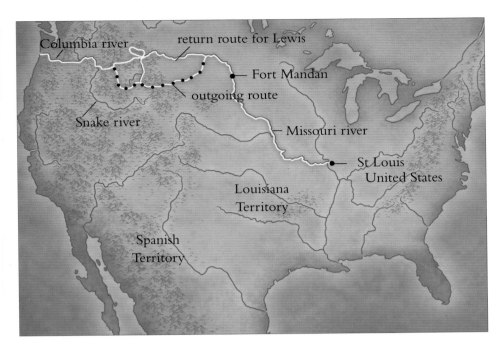

Above: The white line indicates the outward journey. For the return journey the leaders followed different paths.

Montana. They were forced overland. Rejoining the river, by July they had reached the point where it again divides: they called two of the branches Gallatin and Madison, after Jefferson's secretaries of the treasury and state, and followed the third, which they named in honour of the president himself.

The following month the expedition crossed the continental divide and travelled through the mountains in what are now the states of Montana and Idaho. The arduous 11-day journey was a formidable challenge: members of the expedition almost starved, surviving only with help given to them by friendly Native Americans.

On 16 October 1805 they reached the Columbia River, and the following month ended their 6,500km (4,000-mile) journey at the Pacific Ocean. It had taken 554 days. One member had died on the expedition: Charles Floyd had suffered what was probably a ruptured appendix, soon after they had left St Louis. The expedition spent the winter in what is now Oregon, preparing for the journey back across the continent.

RETURN AND AFTERMATH

Lewis and Clark set out on their return journey in March 1806, and it took them another two and a half years to reach home. They had established that Jefferson's idea for a continental route from east to west via the two rivers was not feasible: the Rocky Mountains obstructed the way. Later travellers would go south through Wyoming. The expedition was nevertheless significant in fulfilling Jefferson's other purpose: it had gathered information about the American interior and the West, its native peoples, the topography, fauna and flora. In addition to detailed observations written by both Clark and Lewis, Clark produced maps of the route that became the basis for a more accurate cartography of the West.

Jefferson appointed Meriwether Lewis governor of the Upper Louisiana Territory. William Clark joined him as brigadier general of its militia and Indian agent, and subsequently became governor of the Missouri Territory.

Lewis died in mysterious circumstances in 1809; it is unclear whether he was murdered or took his own life. Clark lived for another 30 years, until his death in St Louis in 1838. The achievements of the expedition were written into American history, demonstrating the pioneer spirit that would infuse a generation of those who followed Lewis and Clark across the continent of the United States.

Below: The expedition survived the harsh conditions because of the help given by friendly native tribes.

JAMES MADISON
1809–1817

If anyone was qualified to be president, James Madison assuredly was. Born in 1751 into a family of well-to-do Virginia planters, he was a graduate of Princeton College in New Jersey. In 1776, aged 25, he first met Thomas Jefferson, and in that year he helped to draft the Virginia Constitution. He was the youngest delegate at the Continental Congress, and after the War of Independence ended he returned to Virginia as a member of its legislature. Formidable in political debate, Madison was personally reticent, the opposite to his extrovert wife, Dolley, whom he married in 1794. Like Washington, Madison had no children.

Madison was the guiding spirit of the Philadelphia Convention, proposing the plan of union, participating in the deliberations over its final form, and even recording the most complete account

Born: 16 March 1751, Port Conway, Virginia
Parents: James (1723–1801) and Eleanor (1731–1829)
Family background: Farming
Education: College of New Jersey (Princeton) (1771)
Religion: Episcopalian
Occupation: Lawyer
Slave owner: Yes
Political career: Virginia Constitutional Convention, 1776
Continental Congress, 1780–3
Virginia State Legislature, 1784–6
Constitutional Convention, 1787
US House of Representatives, 1789–97
Secretary of state, 1801–9
Presidential annual salary: $25,000
Political party: Democrat-Republican
Died: 28 June 1836, Montpelier, Virginia

of its secret deliberations. He helped in the ratification process, contributing to the Federalist Papers and fulfilling the commitment to frame a Bill of Rights, a task that President Washington left to him as a member of the first Federal House of Representatives. After promoting the Republican party's cause in Congress, in 1801 he became Jefferson's secretary of state.

Madison supported the introduction of the Embargo Act, the measure by which Jefferson hoped to curtail the warring British and French blockades of American trade by stopping foreign trade altogether. By 1808 its disastrous economic repercussions were causing widespread discontent in New England, where the act was so unpopular that there was talk of secession, and the

Above: Known as the Father of the Constitution, Madison designed the blueprint for America's republican democracy.

Federalist party, which Jefferson and Madison had worked so hard to destroy, was optimistic about a comeback. But Republicans still managed to dominate the electoral college. Madison, now the leading figure in the Republican party that he had helped to create, defeated Charles Pinckney to become the fourth president of the United States.

EUROPEAN PROBLEMS
The turbulent world of European rivalries shaped the politics of Madison's presidency, as it had shaped those of his predecessors. Madison continued the policy that he and Jefferson had started:

attempting economic warfare against France and Britain so that both might be persuaded to respect the United States' maritime rights. The actions were self-defeating. Congress had repealed the Embargo Act in 1809, but in March that year, just before Madison took office, it again banned trade with the European powers. The following year, it authorized Madison to resume transatlantic commerce on the understanding that if either the French or the British stopped their illegal searches of American merchant ships, trade with the other would cease. Napoleon announced his intention to comply. On 2 November 1810, Madison issued a proclamation resuming trade with France and at the same time stopping American trade with Britain.

In 1811, the threat of war became more of a reality as the continuing conflict with Native American tribes in the Ohio Valley, who had formed an alliance led by the Shawnee chief Tecumseh, escalated. Meanwhile the British continued to ignore the United States' maritime rights as a neutral nation.

In Congress, 'War Hawks' – those from the South and West advocating war with Britain – argued for a more aggressive approach. The president was persuaded, not least because his electoral base was in those two regions. On 1 June 1812, 15 days after he had been nominated for a second term, he sent a message to Congress. The British had committed a "series of acts hostile to the United States as an independent and neutral nation". Just over two weeks later Congress declared war.

CONFLICT AT HOME

Madison's re-election showed that the conflict had increased sectional tensions: New England's transatlantic trade remained disrupted and the war was unpopular there. Madison won by 37 electoral college votes over his opponent, Dewitt Clinton from New York, whose support was concentrated in the New England states bordering the Atlantic.

The conflict with Britain preoccupied the nation until its end in 1814, but a political controversy that

DOLLEY MADISON

Born in May 1768, Dorothea Dandridge Payne Todd was a widow with a two-year-old son when she married James Madison in 1794. She was a vivacious hostess, and began to define the public role of first ladies by associating herself with charitable causes.

Below: Dolley Madison saved Washington's portrait when British troops set fire to the White House during the War of 1812.

stretched back to the first years of the federal republic continued throughout Madison's second term. The charter of the Bank of the United States, which Madison had opposed in 1791, had expired in 1811 and the bank had closed. In 1815, the president vetoed a compromise measure agreed between Republicans and Federalists in Congress that would have allowed it to reopen. However, following the difficulties of financing the War of 1812, the Second National Bank was finally given a 21-year charter in 1816 and opened for business in Philadelphia.

RETIREMENT

Madison retired to Montpelier, his Virginia plantation, succeeding Jefferson as the second rector of the University of Virginia. He died in 1836. His enduring legacies remain the American Constitution and the Bill of Rights.

STATES ENTERING THE UNION DURING MADISON'S PRESIDENCY:

LOUISIANA

Entered the Union: 30 April 1812
Pre-state history: Orleans Territory organized from Louisiana Purchase (1804)
Total population in 1820 census: 153,407
Total number of slaves in 1820 census: 69,064
Electoral College votes in 1812: 3

INDIANA

Entered the Union: 11 December 1816
Pre-state history: Acquired by British (1763); ceded to US (1783); part of Northwest Territory (1787); organized as Indiana Territory (1800)
Total population in 1820 census: 147,178
Total number of slaves in 1820 census: 190
Electoral College votes in 1816: 3

TECUMSEH
SHAWNEE LEADER

Native Americans were generally the losers in the military confrontations that took place in North America in the late 18th and early 19th centuries. Nevertheless, the tactical alliances that different tribes made with the European powers competing for control of the continent made sense, given that expanding settlement in America encroached upon territory they regarded as theirs by right of prior occupation. Having sided with the French during the Seven Years War, and with the British during the War of Independence, Native Americans rejected the new United States government's claims on land to the west of the original colonies and resisted the effort to organize it into new states.

As Lewis and Clark discovered on their journey through the Louisiana Territory, the American continent was

Below: Native Americans fought to prevent the United States taking over their land. In 1794 they were defeated at the Battle of Fallen Timbers.

peopled with many different tribes, or nations, of Native Americans, which like the newly independent states could squabble among themselves as well as unite for the common good. In 1787, the shifting network of alliances among the native peoples of the Ohio Valley consolidated in opposition to US settlement there. When conflict erupted, the regular troops in the United States army, few in number, faced a formidable opposition. In 1791, at Fort Wayne in what is now Indiana, they suffered their heaviest defeat ever at the hands of Native Americans.

The alliance of tribes opposing the United States was weakened when the British, who had supported their cause, withdrew, unannounced, from the Northwest Territory following the signing of the Jay Treaty. In 1794, American troops (including the future president, then Lieutenant William Henry Harrison) prevailed at the Battle of Fallen Timbers, and the following year the Treaty of Greenville forced the tribes to give up their claims to most of

Above: A natural leader, Tecumseh spent his life trying to unite the differing Native American tribes.

what would become the state of Ohio. It was not the end of the matter. In the early 19th century, a Shawnee chief revived the spirit of co-operation between the native tribes and again confronted the Federal government. His name was Tecumseh.

TECUMSEH'S WAR

Born in 1768, Tecumseh had fought at the Battle of Fallen Timbers. Refusing to accept the terms of the Treaty of Greenville, he started to rebuild the confederation of tribes, broadening its support, and by 1808, the year Madison was elected to the White House, he had established a base at Tippecanoe, near Lafayette in the Indiana Territory. His brother, Tenskwatawa, 'The Prophet', was the spiritual leader of the movement. As war fever grew, this revitalized alliance was able to gain the support of the British in Canada.

William Henry Harrison was now governor of the Indiana Territory, and in command of a unit of the US army. He decided to take action. In

November 1811, with Tecumseh absent on one of his many trips to rally support, he and his forces approached Tippecanoe and were confronted by Tenskwatawa. The battle was inconclusive, but Tenskwatawa was disgraced by his lack of success and fled to Canada. The Native Americans subsequently abandoned their headquarters and the alliance broke up.

Tecumseh remained defiant. In the War of 1812 between the United States and Britain, his followers were involved on the British side when the American attempt to invade Canada came to a disastrous end. In October of the following year, however, Tecumseh was killed at the Battle of the Thames, which took place as American forces, once again commanded by William Henry Harrison, pursued the British and their Native American allies during their retreat from Detroit.

AMERICAN EXPANSION

The expansion of the United States westwards across the continent is a defining theme in the nation's history. It is superimposed on an earlier migration that took place from north to south as, during the Ice Age, those who would become Native Americans walked across a land bridge over the

Bering Strait from Asia. Later arrivals, from the 15th century onwards, brought with them different cultures and traditions, which ultimately proved incompatible with Native American life.

Colonial America was organized into settlements, towns, cities and eventually the United States. Native American tribes had an alternative sense of the land, which was nomadic and recognized only natural borders. Moreover, the sheer numbers who came from Europe to America meant that the population expanded rapidly. By 1810

Above: Tecumseh was fatally shot in the War of 1812 at the Battle of the Thames in Canada. With his death, the union of Native American tribes disintegrated.

more than a million people lived west of the Appalachian Mountains. Native Americans, diminished through disease and war, tried to resist the settlement of the West. Like Tecumseh, however, they fought a losing battle.

Below: American settlers claimed the land once occupied by Native Americans.

THE WAR WITH BRITAIN
1812

As his term of office came to an end in 1797 George Washington knew that the United States was neither economically nor militarily strong enough to fight a war with Britain. He thought that conflict should be avoided "for about 20 years". The War of 1812 arrived more or less on cue, but for the United States, a politically divided nation, it was still a risky undertaking.

There were a number of reasons for the conflict. Britain's press-ganging of American sailors to fight against the French, as well as the imposition of trade restrictions across the Atlantic, had caused outrage in the United States. British attempts to stir up unrest among Native American tribes in the Midwest added fuel to such resentment, and some Americans saw an opportunity to expel the British governors from Canada: the pro-war 'hawks' in Congress argued that this would be another war for American independence.

The war was fought on three fronts: in Canada and the Great Lakes, at sea in the Atlantic Ocean, and in the South and West of America where American forces confronted hostile tribes of Native Americans.

WAR IN CANADA

Early American hopes of annexing Canada from Britain proved misplaced. The United States attempted to invade from three different directions: from Detroit into Upper Canada, where the absence of British troops and the presence of US settlers was thought to guarantee success; across the border at Niagara; and from Lake Champlain towards Montreal. One after another these attacks failed.

In August 1812, the British forced an American retreat and captured Detroit. In October the United States lost the Battle of Queenstown Heights on the Niagara River, and the following month

they withdrew from Lake Champlain without confronting the British. US fortunes turned when, on the Great Lakes, Captain Oliver Perry's victory in the Battle of Lake Erie in September 1813 forced the British to abandon Detroit. A second invasion of Canada culminated in the Battle of the Thames on 5 October, in which the US forces were victorious.

WAR IN THE ATLANTIC

In January 1814, Madison asked a visitor from Britain to sum up British public opinion on the war. The reply was revealing: "Half the people ... do not know there is a war with America, and those who did have forgotten it." From a British perspective, the pre-eminent concern remained its military struggle with France in Europe rather than the conflict in America. In April 1814, Napoleon abdicated and the following month another Treaty of Paris temporarily ended the fighting in Europe. Britain refocused its energies across the Atlantic in America.

The US navy, whose exploits were symbolized by the USS *Constitution*, proved better equipped and better led than its British counterpart, while American privateers successfully harassed British merchant ships, but the first attack in the war in the Atlantic surprised the United States. It came in

Left: The burning of Washington had a significant effect in curbing the public's enthusiasm for war.

August 1814 via Chesapeake Bay, where British forces met with little opposition and advanced on Washington DC. The president was among those forced hurriedly to leave town, and the Capitol building and the White House were set ablaze. The British continued to Baltimore, but failed to take the city and withdrew. The United States' humiliation was partially redeemed, and it was

'OLD IRONSIDES'

USS *Constitution*, the American navy's oldest commissioned ship, was made of oak, but received its nickname, 'Old Ironsides', because its sides were proof against enemy cannonballs. One of six frigates that made up the original navy, it was built in Boston in 1797, equipped with 44 guns and carried a crew of over 450. During the War of 1812, it defeated British ships in battles off the coasts of the United States and Brazil. It last saw combat in 1815. Fifteen years later it was scheduled for the scrap yard, but a celebratory poem by Oliver Wendell Holmes led to a successful public campaign to preserve it as part of the nation's naval heritage.

Below: The USS Constitution.

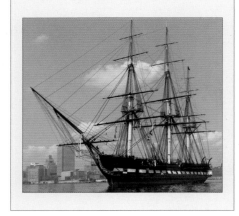

Above: Oliver H. Perry, officer of the United States navy, led a decisive victory at the Battle of Lake Erie.

the fight to defend Baltimore that inspired Francis Scott Key to compose what became America's anthem, "The Star Spangled Banner".

DISSENSION IN THE STATES

In New York, from Lake Champlain and down the Hudson River, war also raged. The British aimed to isolate New England from the rest of the United States. New Hampshire, Connecticut and Massachusetts had already refused to support the American war effort and among those states where its economic impact was most acutely felt there was growing opposition to the war. In September 1814, at the Battle of Plattsburgh on Lake Champlain, the British were defeated and retreated to Canada, but at the Hartford Convention in December, New Englanders talked of secession if the war continued.

However, both sides had wearied of the fight. The Treaty of Ghent, which ended hostilities, was negotiated by, among others, a future president, John Quincy Adams, and was signed on

Right: Andrew Jackson's military exploits during the War of 1812 made him a national hero.

Christmas Eve, 1814. Before it was ratified by the Senate the following month, a final act of war was played out by another future chief executive: Andrew Jackson.

ANDREW JACKSON'S WAR

The third element of the British strategy involved a blockade of the Mississippi at New Orleans. Here they encountered Andrew Jackson, who during the war had spent his time in the South leading an army that fought brutal campaigns and seized land from Native Americans, the Spanish and the British. By December 1814, he had occupied New Orleans. On 8 January 1815, unaware that the peace treaty had been signed, the British tried to capture

THE HARTFORD CONVENTION

The trading economies of the New England states had been badly affected before hostilities broke out in 1812 by British harassment of US merchant ships and the backfiring of the Embargo Act. The Federalist party, which opposed 'Mr Madison's War', exploited this sectional discontent. In October 1814, representatives from Massachusetts, Connecticut, Rhode Island, New Hampshire and Vermont met in Hartford, Connecticut. They considered, but rejected, the idea of secession. Suggested Constitutional amendments were agreed and a delegation sent to Washington to present them to the federal government. It arrived after the war had been won, fatally undermining its protest. The Federalist party never recovered and within four years had been destroyed as a political and electoral force.

the city, but Jackson fought a swift and decisive battle, with few American casualties, and emerged victorious.

If the War of Independence made Washington an inevitable choice for president, Andrew Jackson, the hero of New Orleans, similarly used his military reputation to advance a political career that would lead him to the White House.

JAMES MONROE
1817–1825

Born in 1758, James Monroe was the last president to be elected who, as a young man, had been directly involved in the struggle for American independence. While at William and Mary College, he had helped to steal British weapons, giving them to the Virginia militia. In 1776, aged 18, as an officer in the Continental Army, he was severely wounded at the Battle of Trenton.

After the war Monroe studied law under Jefferson's guidance, then entered politics in 1783, as a representative in the Continental Congress. He married Elizabeth Kortright in 1785. Two daughters survived to adulthood, and a son died before the age of two.

Losing out to Madison in elections to the new federal House of Representatives, Monroe was appointed instead to the Senate. After serving as America's representative in Paris he became

Born: 28 April 1758, Westmoreland County, Virginia
Parents: Spence (? –1774) and Elizabeth (?)
Family background: Farming
Education: William and Mary College (1776)
Religion: Episcopalian
Occupation: Lawyer
Slave owner: Yes
Political career: Continental Congress, 1783–6
United States Senate, 1790–4
Minister to France, 1794–6
Governor of Virginia, 1799–1802
Minister to France and England, 1803–7
Secretary of state, 1811–17
Secretary of war, 1814–15
Presidential annual salary: $25,000
Political party: Democrat-Republican
Died: 4 July 1831, New York

governor of Virginia in 1799. He returned to France to negotiate the Louisiana Purchase and remained in Europe as a diplomat for four years, serving in Britain and Spain. He was again briefly Virginia's governor before joining Madison's administration as secretary of state and also as secretary of war. By 1816, Monroe was Madison's obvious successor, winning a convincing victory over Rufus King, from New York, in the electoral college.

GOODWILL ERA BEGINS
Monroe worked hard to overcome sectional and party tensions. His cabinet included John Calhoun from South Carolina and John Quincy Adams from Massachusetts. Henry Clay from

Above: James Monroe presided in a period of relative political calm. His presidency embraced the "Era of Good Feelings".

Kentucky might also have joined the administration but preferred to remain in Congress. The inclusion of Adams who, like his father, was a Federalist, as secretary of state demonstrated that its leading members no longer considered the party a vehicle for their political ambitions: indeed, even its name was no longer much used.

The new president imitated Washington, embarking on a national goodwill tour. A Boston newspaper described his presence in the city as marking the start of an "Era of Good Feelings" for the whole United States.

In 1818, General Andrew Jackson,
combating raids into Georgia by Native
American tribes from Spanish Florida,
invaded that territory and in so doing
demonstrated the weakness of Spain's
control over its North American possessions. Spain protested, but did not
have the means to retaliate, or retake the
territory by force. Adams was able to
negotiate a treaty with Spain by which
the United States acquired Florida in
return for payment of five million
dollars, and the Mexican border was
extended to the Pacific Ocean.

In February 1819, as an economic
downturn started to sour the political
atmosphere, slavery again caused controversy. The border between slave and
non-slave states was defined by the
Mason–Dixon line. Missouri, which like
other slave states lay to its south, had
applied to join the Union. An
amendment prohibiting slavery was
added to the bill giving it statehood,
even though there were already slaves
there. As Congress wrestled with this
problem, mindful that if Missouri
entered the Union the balance between
slave and non-slave states – at that time
there were 11 of each – would be upset,
Monroe gave his support to the creation

STATES JOINING THE UNION DURING MONROE'S PRESIDENCY:

MISSISSIPPI

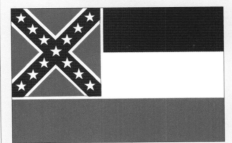

Entered the Union: 10 December
1817
Pre-state history: Organized as
American territory (1798) and
expanded (1804 and 1812)
**Total population in 1820
census:** 75,440
**Total number of slaves in 1820
census:** 32,814
Electoral College votes in 1820: 2

ILLINOIS

Entered the Union: 3 December 1818
Pre-state history: Acquired by British
(1763); ceded to US (1783); part of
Northwest Territory (1787); organized
as Illinois Territory (1809)
**Total population in 1820
census:** 55,211
**Total number of slaves in 1820
census:** 917
Electoral College votes in 1820: 3

ALABAMA

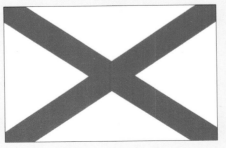

Entered the Union: 14 December 1819
Pre-state history: Part of Mississippi
Territory (1798); western portion
became Mississippi, eastern portion
organized as Alabama Territory (1817)
**Total population in 1820
census:** 144,317
**Total number of slaves in 1820
census:** 47,449
Electoral College votes in 1820: 3

MAINE

Entered the Union: 15 March 1820
Pre-state history: Part of
Massachusetts; became independent
state through Missouri Compromise
**Total population in 1820
census:** 298,335
**Total number of slaves in 1820
census:** 0
Electoral College votes in 1820: 9

MISSOURI

Entered the Union: 10 August 1821
Pre-state history: Part of Louisiana
Territory, renamed Missouri Territory
following Louisiana's admission to the
union (1812)
**Total population in 1820
census:** 66,586
**Total number of slaves in 1820
census:** 10,222
Electoral College votes in 1820: 3

of a West African colony where freed slaves could be repatriated. In 1824, when Liberia was established, its capital was named Monrovia.

Meanwhile, Henry Clay emerged as the political fixer, engineering the Missouri Compromise (1820). Under its terms Maine was created from the northernmost parts of Massachusetts and admitted as a free state, while Missouri became the twelfth slave-holding state in the union. No further extension of slavery was permitted to its north and west.

In the 1820 election, Monroe was unopposed. However, one member of the electoral college with a sense of history voted instead for John Quincy Adams, so that George Washington would remain the only president to be elected unanimously.

SECOND TERM

At the beginning of the 19th century the Spanish Empire was in decline, not only in North but also in South America. In 1822, following the acquisition of Florida, Monroe extended diplomatic recognition to Argentina, Chile, Colombia and Mexico, which had all freed themselves of Spanish imperial rule. In 1823, when it appeared that Spain might attempt to rebuild its empire to the south, the president set out what subsequently became known as the Monroe Doctrine (see opposite). As his second term came to an end, the "Era of Good Feelings" disintegrated, and Monroe's colleagues jockeyed to succeed him. The president refused to name his preferred candidate. The result was an acrimonious and disputed election in 1824.

RETIREMENT

Monroe lived for only six years after he left office. Like John Adams and Thomas Jefferson, he died as the nation celebrated the day that marked its Declaration of Independence. The 'Virginia Dynasty' was at an end.

THE MASON–DIXON LINE

Above: The boundary lines established by Mason and Dixon remain legal boundaries today.

The original boundary line was drawn by Charles Mason and Jeremiah Dixon, two British surveyors called in after a legal ruling had settled the disputed boundary between two British colonies. They established the east–west border between Pennsylvania and Maryland, beginning their work in 1763 and completing it four years and 375km (233 miles) later. As a result of the Missouri Compromise in 1820, the Mason–Dixon line was

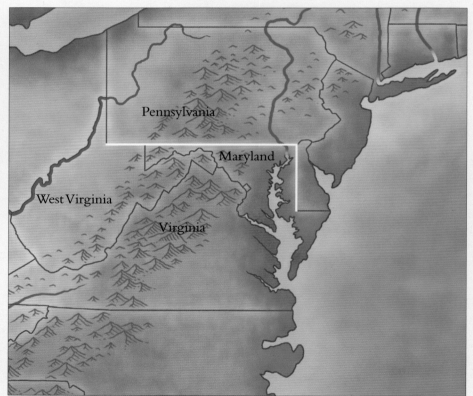

extended west to the Ohio river, then to the Mississippi, and finally along a latitude 36 degrees west and 30 minutes north. It became the popular description of the boundary between Northern free states and those in the South where slavery was permitted.

Above: The Mason–Dixon line resolved the boundary dispute between Maryland and Pennsylvania over ownership of land between the 39th and 40th parallels. Both states claimed it for their own. The new boundary was marked every mile with stones.

THE MONROE DOCTRINE
1823

Left: Monroe with his Cabinet: the Monroe Doctrine became one of the foundation stones of American foreign policy.

The Monroe Doctrine, which outlined the foreign policy of the United States in the hemisphere of the Americas, was outlined in the president's annual message to Congress on 2 December 1823. There had been widespread concern that an alliance of European powers including France and Spain once more had designs on America. The British foreign minister, George Canning, had suggested that the United States join Britain in a declaration that would make clear their opposition to any such intervention.

Monroe's two predecessors advised him that this was a good idea. Jefferson wrote to him in October that the issue was: "the most momentous … since that of Independence. That made us a nation, this sets our compass and points the course which we are to steer thro' the ocean of time opening on us."

John Quincy Adams thought differently. He persuaded Monroe that the United States should act alone, and helped to draft the message to Congress in which the president made clear that the Americas – North and South – were not there to be colonized by Europe. "We should consider any attempt on their part to extend their system to any portion of this hemisphere as dangerous to our peace and safety." Europe should not meddle in the Americas' business and neither would the United States be concerned with Europe's internal rivalries.

The Monroe Doctrine had no real force: the United States was not yet strong enough to resist European military power. For the next century, it would rely upon British sea power to help deter other European nations that might have imperial ambitions across the Atlantic. American and British interests coincided, not for the last time. The Americans wanted to preserve their independence and the British, having accepted the loss of their colonies in the New World, did not want rival powers to supplant them.

NEIGHBOURS TO THE SOUTH

Initially, Monroe's statement suggested that the United States had much in common with the republics that had fought for their independence from Spain, just as the Americans had successfully resisted the British. But in time, as the United States became more powerful, it ignored the principle of non-interference outlined in the doctrine as it sought to influence the politics of its neighbours to the south.

Below: "That's a live wire, gentlemen." Uncle Sam warns John Bull and Kaiser Wilhelm not to transgress US territory.

CHAPTER THREE

JOHN QUINCY ADAMS TO JAMES POLK

1824–1848

IT WAS 'THE AGE OF JACKSON'. THE MILITARY HERO LOST TO JOHN QUINCY ADAMS IN 1824, BUT BECAME THE FIGUREHEAD OF A NEW PARTY, THE DEMOCRATS, WHICH SWEPT HIM INTO OFFICE FOUR YEARS LATER. 'OLD HICKORY', AS HE WAS KNOWN, WAS THE ONLY PRESIDENT DURING THIS TIME TO BE RE-ELECTED. THE WHIG PARTY, NAMED AFTER ITS BRITISH ANTI-MONARCHICAL COUNTERPART, CONFRONTED 'KING ANDREW' AND IN 1840 DEFEATED HIS DEMOCRAT SUCCESSOR, MARTIN VAN BUREN. WHIGS OCCUPIED THE WHITE HOUSE FOR JUST FOUR YEARS: WILLIAM HENRY HARRISON BECAME THE FIRST PRESIDENT TO DIE IN OFFICE, AND JOHN TYLER LOST IN 1844 TO JAMES POLK, WHOSE TIES TO JACKSON EARNED HIM THE NICKNAME 'YOUNG HICKORY'. THE ERA ENDED WITH THE NATION STILL ADDING TO ITS TERRITORY, BUT WITH THE PROBLEM OF SLAVERY UNRESOLVED.

Left: Andrew Jackson at the Battle of New Orleans,
the last major battle of the War of 1812.

THE PRESIDENTIAL ELECTION

1824

Four years after the Federalist party had been unable to offer even token opposition to the re-election of President Monroe, the political momentum of Democratic-Republicanism, first represented by Thomas Jefferson, and which had carried all before it during the 'Era of Good Feelings' stalled under the leadership of James Monroe. So one era ended and another began. Once more the outcome of a presidential election was to be decided in the House of Representatives. This time, it was John Quincy Adams, the son of Jefferson's defeated opponent in 1800, who would emerge victorious.

Initially there were five candidates, one from the North (Adams), two from the South (Crawford and Calhoun) and two from the West (Clay and Jackson).

Adams, the New Englander, was then secretary of state and the leading contender. His politics agreed with those of Henry Clay, the congressman from Kentucky and the broker of the Missouri Compromise, but Clay harboured presidential ambitions of his own. William Crawford, from Georgia, was Monroe's secretary of the treasury, and John Calhoun, from South Carolina, was his secretary for war. Then there was Andrew Jackson.

Underestimated by all his rivals, who viewed him as an irascible rabble-rouser, Jackson, then a senator from Tennessee, managed to win outright in eight states and gained a majority of the electoral college in three others. With the support of one representative from New York, he eventually won 99 electoral college

votes in 12 states. Not all states elected representatives to the electoral college – some still used their legislatures to nominate them – but Jackson also won the greatest number of the popular votes cast.

Adams came second. He won the entire support of six states and additional electoral college votes in five others, including a majority in New York, to reach a total of 84. Crawford had the support of only his home state and Virginia, but his 41 electoral college votes meant that he still beat Henry

Below: The presidential candidates in the 1824 election were favoured in different parts of the country. The race for the presidency was based on personality rather than policy.

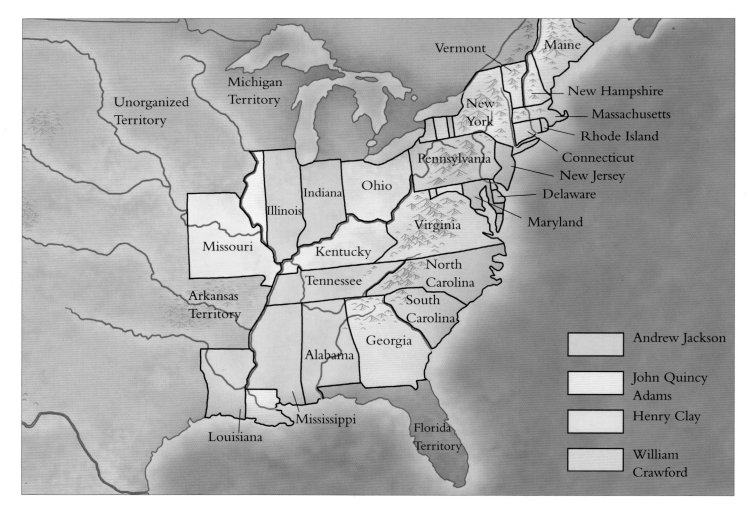

Above: John Quincy Adams.

Above: William Crawford.

Above: John Calhoun.

Clay, with 37, into last place. Calhoun had withdrawn his candidacy and won the vice-presidential contest convincingly instead.

THE 'CORRUPT BARGAIN'

No candidate had the required electoral college majority of 131 votes. The next step was clear. The revised rules for electing the president, agreed in the Twelfth Amendment to the Constitution, meant that the final choice was between the top three candidates: Jackson, Adams and Crawford. The 24 states in which the election had been fought now had just one vote each in the House of Representatives to determine the outcome. Henry Clay, whose name did not go forward, still had a role to play in his capacity as Speaker of the House and gave his support to Adams.

On 9 February 1825, the House of Representatives chose John Adams on the first ballot. He won the support of 13 states, to Jackson's seven and Crawford's four. Adams had retained the support of the six states in which he had won outright in the electoral college, as well as New York, where he had been the overwhelming favourite. He gained the votes of Illinois and Louisiana, where in the election he had run a close second to Jackson. Maryland, which on the basis of its votes in the first stage of the election might have

supported Jackson, now switched to Adams. The three states making up the rest of his majority, Kentucky, Ohio and Missouri, were all in the gift of the candidate who had won them in the electoral college: Henry Clay.

The journal of the House of Representatives records that, when the outcome of the election was announced, "some clapping and exultation took place in the galleries, and some slight hissing followed. The House suspended its proceedings until the galleries were cleared."

Rumours circulated that Clay and Adams had made a 'corrupt bargain', and that in return for his support Adams would offer Clay his choice of

Below: Henry Clay.

position in the new administration. The suspicion was apparently confirmed when soon afterwards Clay, the Speaker of the House, became secretary of state. Jackson resigned from the Senate in protest at the result.

The election, in which 18 of the 24 states had allowed popular participation in the selection of representatives to the electoral college, had ended amid accusations that this more open and democratic process had been hijacked by establishment politicians, deciding matters behind closed doors. Jackson exploited this sentiment, and four years later, like many future candidates, ran 'against Washington' in his successful campaign for the White House.

Below: Andrew Jackson.

JOHN QUINCY ADAMS
1825–1829

John Quincy Adams grew up during the era of independence and revolution, witnessing the Battle of Bunker Hill three months before his eighth birthday. He followed, literally, in his father's footsteps, accompanying John Adams on diplomatic trips abroad, graduating at the same age from Harvard, and also initially pursuing a career as a lawyer.

George Washington started Adams's career in public service, sending him to represent the United States in Holland, and his diplomatic career in Europe continued during his father's presidency. While in London, in 1797, he married Louisa Johnson, the daughter of the American consul there. Shortly afterwards, he was posted to Prussia, returning to the United States after Thomas Jefferson won the 1800 election. In 1801 the first of his four

Born: 11 July 1767, Braintree (now Quincy), Massachusetts
Parents: John (1735–1826) and Abigail (1744–1818)
Family background: Law, politics
Education: Harvard College (1787)
Religion: Episcopalian
Occupation: Lawyer
Slave owner: No
Political career: Minister to the Netherlands, 1794
Minister to Prussia, 1797–1801
United States Senate, 1803–8
Minister to Russia, 1809–11
Peace commissioner: Treaty of Ghent, 1814
Secretary of state, 1817–25
House of Representatives, 1831–48
Presidential annual salary: $25,000
Political party: Democrat-Republican
Died: 23 February 1848, Washington DC

Above: The election debacle created mistrust of John Quincy Adams, who suffered from a lack of support for his domestic reforms.

children, named for George Washington, was born and in the same year he entered the federal Senate.

In the shifting party politics of the time, Adams gravitated from his father's party towards the Jeffersonian Republicans. In 1807 he supported the Embargo Act, alienating both the Federalists and his Massachusetts constituency. Having resigned from the Senate when Madison came to the White House, Adams took up a succession of diplomatic posts in Europe, witnessing Napoleon's invasion of Russia in 1812 and helping to negotiate the peace treaty between America and Britain. He won the election of 1824 at 57, four years younger than his father had been when he became president.

TAINTED ADMINISTRATION

"The spirit of improvement is abroad upon the earth" was the message of Adams's first annual message to Congress. Despite the circumstances surrounding his election, he assumed a mandate to propose an ambitious programme of public works aimed at improving the transport infrastructure of the United States. Roads and canals were the nation's arteries of trade, and better communications encouraged Americans to travel and settle across the continent. He also suggested that a national university should be established as part of his ambition to promote the arts and scientific knowledge. In many ways he appeared to be returning to his Federalist roots, believing that it was the role of the national government to take the lead in developing the nation's resources, economy and wealth.

Adams's independence of thought and aloofness of manner did not win him political friends, and the 'corrupt bargain' accusation tainted his administration from the start. John Calhoun, his vice president, was among those who were convinced that Adams and Clay had connived to deny the popular choice, Andrew Jackson, the presidency. In Calhoun's opinion it was "the most dangerous stab which the liberty of this country has ever received". As Adams's popularity declined, he could no longer rely on the support of Congress, which

in 1828 passed a new Tariff Act, aimed at protecting northern manufacturers and western agricultural products through setting high rates of duty on imports. In the South this 'Tariff of Abominations' was condemned as unjust and unconstitutional, and Adams, who had signed it into law reluctantly, was blamed.

Later that year he stood for re-election. Calhoun, who throughout the administration had conspired with Adams's political adversaries, openly supported Jackson, while continuing in office as vice president. Adams received only one less electoral college vote than he had four years previously, but this time, with Jackson as his only opponent, the incumbent president suffered a comprehensive defeat.

AFTER THE PRESIDENCY

On leaving the White House, Adams enhanced his reputation among those arguing for the abolition of slavery through his implacable opposition to the South's 'peculiar institution'. Two years after his retirement he returned to Washington as a member of the House of Representatives, the only ex-president to be elected to Congress. He famously argued the 'Amistad Case' before the Supreme Court.

Adams spent the remaining 18 years of his life as a congressman. He campaigned relentlessly and ultimately

successfully for the repeal of the 'gag rules', passed by Southerners in the years before the Civil War to prevent the discussion of anti-slavery petitions. In 1846 he was a leading opponent of the war with Mexico.

Following a lifetime of public service, it was fitting that, on 23 February 1848, Adams died, aged 80, in the Speaker's Room, after suffering a stroke in the chamber of the House itself. He was the last survivor of that generation of prominent politicians whose lives encompassed the fight for independence, the creation of the United States, and the challenges it faced during its first 60 years as a democratic republic.

POLITICAL PARTIES
AND THEIR APPEAL TO THE ELECTORATE

By the early years of the 19th century the Federalists had disappeared. The Republicans, led by Jefferson, Madison and Monroe, who had renamed themselves Democrat-Republicans, became the all-inclusive political vehicle that drove Jefferson and his compatriots in the 'Virginia Dynasty' to the White House. The Democrat-Republicans were the only party capable of nominating candidates for office by 1820, but four years later they had fragmented. By 1828 the party was irretrievably divided.

During Andrew Jackson's presidency, a more durable party system began to emerge. Andrew Jackson's Democrat

Below: The view of the Capitol from the White House, 1840.

party, egalitarian, expansionist and populist in its appeal to small landowners and working-class labourers, was opposed from the 1830s onwards by the Whigs, the party of commercial and manufacturing interests. Within 20 years, however, the Whigs too would be swept away by a political wave identifying itself with America's past and adopting a very familiar name: the Republican party.

Party competition in the United States re-emerged through a complex alchemy of personalities, competing sectional priorities and two continuing political arguments: what should be the extent of the federal government's powers and how could the issue of slavery be resolved?

THE IMPORTANCE OF
ANDREW JACKSON

The catalyst for the development of the Democrat party was Andrew Jackson. Following his defeat in 1824, his supporters built a grass-roots coalition that enabled him to win the presidency four years later. The organizational genius behind it was Senator Martin Van Buren from New York, but it was Jackson's status as a national military hero, coupled with the widespread sentiment that he had been cheated by the 'corrupt bargain' between Adams and Clay in 1824, that made him an irresistible candidate.

Other developments helped Jackson. By 1828, congressional representatives in Washington no longer chose

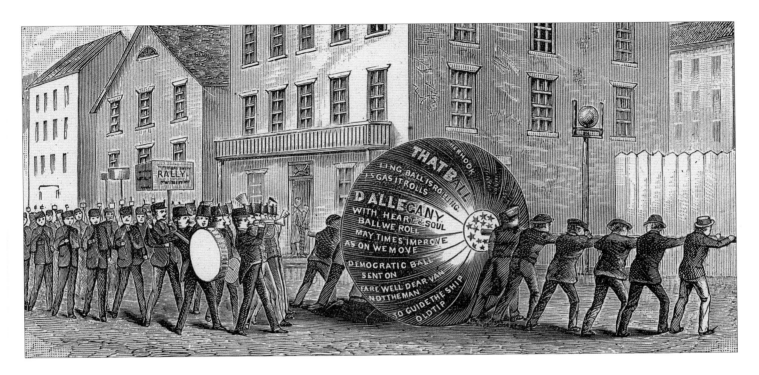

presidential candidates: instead the candidates were nominated by state conventions or in state legislatures. Although the suffrage was still restricted to white men, the right to vote had been extended through the abolition of property qualifications. The new voters had greater opportunities for democratic participation as most states moved towards popular elections for state offices and the electoral college. For Jackson, the symbolism of running as an outsider 'against Washington' had an enormous electoral appeal.

Political labels were still confusing: in 1828 Jacksonians co-opted the old party name, calling themselves Democratic-Republican. Adams reinvented himself as the candidate of the National Republicans. Whatever they were called, the core constituencies of both political groupings were still based in different geographical sections of the nation. Adams's support was in the old Federalist stronghold of New England. Jackson's was overwhelmingly in the South and West, although with Van Buren on the ticket, the Democratic-Republicans won New York. They were also victorious in Pennsylvania.

The 1828 election was the second round in the fight that had broken out within Jefferson's Democrat-Republican party, which had held on to power so tenaciously since 1800. The contest continued as the 'Age of Jackson' took shape, but by 1836 the party that had fragmented from the Republicans, and was now known simply as the Democrats, faced a more organized challenge to its political supremacy.

THE WHIGS

By the end of Jackson's administration, the personal rivalries that had characterized presidential politics for the previous 12 years had played out. John Quincy Adams was in the House of Representatives. Henry Clay, defeated by Jackson in 1832, was in the Senate, and so too was John Calhoun after his resignation as vice president at the end of that year. The 1836 presidential election pitted Calhoun's successor, Van Buren, against opposition from a newly formed party. The Whigs were a disparate coalition, united in their dislike of everything Jacksonian. The first time they challenged the Democrats, they fielded three candidates: two from the South and one from the North. By 1840, however, they had learnt the new realities of presidential politics, nominating William Henry Harrison, a

Above: Harrison was the hero of the Battle of Tippecanoe. His procession marched in triumph to Washington.

Virginia-born patrician whose father had signed the Declaration of Independence, and presenting him as another Jackson: a former general, war hero and rough-hewn frontiersman. This strategy worked and in 1836 the Whigs won the White House.

THE POLITICS OF SLAVERY

As the Democrats became increasingly identified with the slave-owning South, the anti-slavery and abolitionist movement organized politically: after 1854 many Whigs, including Abraham Lincoln, joined the new Republican party. The American party system, emerging from the clash of personalities and competing visions of the powers that should be exercised by federal and state governments, now coalesced around the fundamental faultline of slavery. By the 1860s, the compromises that had been managed in earlier times were no longer possible, as the political parties became increasingly identified with pro-slavery or abolitionist sentiment and war loomed between the states.

ANDREW JACKSON
1829–1837

In 1767, a few weeks after his father's death, Andrew Jackson, the son of first-generation Irish immigrants, was born in a small settlement on the border between North and South Carolina. He was four months older than his predecessor as president, but their early lives could not have been more different. While the teenage John Quincy Adams accompanied his father on diplomatic missions in Europe, Andrew Jackson was acquiring a taste for war in America's fight for independence. He was captured by the British in 1781, and later released in a prisoner exchange. Before the war ended his two elder brothers and his mother had all died. Jackson was 15.

Jackson's education was rudimentary, but he qualified as a frontier lawyer, practising in Nashville, in territory that would later become the state of Tennessee. He embarked on a successful career acquiring land and slaves. In 1791 he married Rachel Donelson Robards, whose father had been one of Nashville's founders.

Born: 15 March 1767, Waxhaw, South Carolina
Parents: Andrew (1730?–67) and Elizabeth (1740?–81)
Family background: Farming
Education: Not formally educated
Religion: Presbyterian
Occupation: Lawyer, soldier
Slave owner: Yes
Political career: US House of Representatives, 1796–7
US Senate, 1797–8, 1823–5
Tennessee Supreme Court judge, 1798–1804
Governor of Florida Territory, 1821
Presidential annual salary: $25,000
Political party: Democrat
Died: 8 June 1845, The Hermitage, Nashville, Tennessee

THE PATH TO THE PRESIDENCY
Jackson's career was spent aggressively adding to US territory, whether invading and occupying Florida to the south, or forcing Native American removal along the 'Trail of Tears' from Georgia to the west. He represented the traditions of the slave-holding South and the opportunism of the expanding West. He settled in Tennessee, which, when it was admitted to the Union in 1796, joined those states south of the Mason–Dixon line while remaining part of the US frontier. He himself owned and traded slaves: in the 1820s he had more than 100 of them.

When Tennessee achieved statehood, Jackson served in both the federal House of Representatives and the

Above: Andrew Jackson, the military hero, swept to victory in the 1828 election, such was the popular sense of injustice at his losing that of 1824.

Senate, before returning to a position on the state's Supreme Court. In 1802, he beat Tennessee's first governor, John Sevier, to become commander of the state militia; it was an acrimonious election, which led to Jackson challenging his opponent to a duel. Two years later, having resigned from the Court, he bought the Hermitage, his plantation near Nashville. He lived privately for eight years, during and after the War of 1812, before using his military successes to relaunch his career on a national platform.

RACHEL JACKSON

Rachel Donelson was born in 1767. Her marriage to Jackson in 1791 was the subject of vitriolic attacks during his 1828 presidential campaign, when rumours about her first marriage and the timing of her divorce were reported in the press. Her husband blamed his enemies for her death two months before he took office. The Jacksons had no children. Emily Donelson, Jackson's niece, was his official hostess until her early death in 1836, the year before he left the White House.

Jackson led the Tennessee Militia in campaigns against Native American tribes to acquire their land, and his victory over the British at the Battle of New Orleans gave him a hero's reputation, but he remained a military maverick. Later on, more ruthless and effective campaigns against native tribes culminated in his effective annexation of Florida from Spanish control, and he became military governor of the Florida Territory in 1821.

On his resignation from the army he returned to Tennessee, and had his political plans turned out as expected, becoming a senator for the second time in 1823 would have been merely a prelude to his election to the presidency a year later. But John Quincy Adams and Henry Clay had other ideas and Jackson resigned once more, returning home to wait. His revenge in 1828 was comprehensive: he received more than twice as many electoral college votes as the incumbent president.

Jackson's wife died three weeks after the results were declared. Like Thomas Jefferson, he was a widower when he entered the White House. Older than any of his predecessors, he took office 11 days before his 62nd birthday.

Right: Americans rushed to the White House to witness the inauguration of their popular hero Andrew Jackson.

SCANDAL AND CONSPIRACY

Throughout his life, Jackson squabbled, fought and occasionally duelled with his political enemies. On becoming president he rewarded his friends, effectively introducing an aspect of United States government that became known as the 'Spoils System': appointees of the former administration lost their positions and Jackson's supporters were given jobs. He also relied on his 'Kitchen Cabinet' – his close friends

Left: Jackson being abandoned by the Cabinet after the 'Peggy Eaton Affair'.

and cronies – for political advice. Early in his administration, his loyalty to one of them, John Eaton, whom he appointed war secretary, caused a scandal in Washington. Eaton's wife Peggy, with whom he had lived before they were married and who was rumoured to have had a colourful private life, was shunned by polite Washington society, notably the wives of the other members of his Cabinet. The vice president's wife, Floride Calhoun, stayed away from the federal capital in case she and Peggy might meet. Jackson convinced himself that what might have begun as moral condemnation was a political conspiracy. In 1831, the ramifications of the 'Peggy Eaton Affair' culminated in Jackson sacking most of his Cabinet. The rift between president and vice president widened. Calhoun did not run for re-election with Jackson in 1832 and resigned in December that year, the month after the election took place.

There was some substance to the president's suspicions. In 1830, Jackson learnt that 12 years previously Calhoun

Above: The first ever assassination attempt on a president was in 1830, while Jackson was attending a funeral.

had been among those in favour of pursuing disciplinary action against him for exceeding his military authority in invading Florida. Earlier that same year the two had clashed when the vice president suggested that his home state of South Carolina could unilaterally ignore a federal tariff on cotton. The doctrine of nullification, which Calhoun had first advanced in protest against the 'Tariff of Abominations' in South Carolina, implied that a state could defy the federal government. For Jackson, nullification meant the potential break-up of the Union, which he was adamant had to be preserved.

DISSENSION IN THE SOUTH

In December 1832, Jackson issued a 'Proclamation to the People of South Carolina', challenging that state's rejection of the 1828 and 1832 Tariff Acts. Persistent clashes between states' rights and federal authority could only have one outcome: "If this doctrine had been established at an earlier day, the Union would have been dissolved in its infancy ... You must perceive that the crisis your conduct presents at this day would recur whenever any law of the United States displeased any of the

Right: A political cartoon of Jackson demanding public money be reclaimed from the National Bank.

States, and that we should soon cease to be a nation." His proclamation came a month after he had been re-elected. South Carolina's support had proved unnecessary as Jackson comprehensively defeated another of those whom he thought had conspired to deprive him of the presidency eight years previously: Henry Clay.

Following his victory, the president threatened to use force to collect the duties that Calhoun's home state had refused to pay and to arrest and hang the leaders of the nullification movement. Congress supported him,

passing the so-called 'Force Act'. It was his defeated opponent who defused the nullification crisis by negotiating a new compromise tariff, just before Jackson was re-inaugurated in March 1833.

Native Americans and the National Bank were not so sacrosanct. In May 1830, the Indian Removal Act cleared the way for the resettlement of tribes to reservations on land to the west of the Mississippi River. Jackson ignored the Supreme Court's ruling that Cherokee Indian land in Georgia was sovereign territory where state laws did not apply, allegedly declaring: "John Marshall [chief justice of the Supreme Court] has made his decision, now let him enforce it!" The Cherokees were forced to migrate from Georgia along the 'Trail of Tears' to Oklahoma.

In the same year, Jackson also vented his longstanding opposition to the National Bank, by vetoing the Act of Congress re-chartering it. "We can at least take a stand", he argued, "against all new grants of monopolies and exclusive privileges". The director of the Bank, Nicholas Biddle, denounced the President's veto message as "a manifesto of anarchy" reminiscent of the declarations that incited mob rule in the aftermath of the French Revolution. Nevertheless, it was Jackson who proved politically astute, even if his grasp of the economics of banking was somewhat shaky. The Bank became an important

THE STATUS OF TEXAS

On 2 March 1836, American settlers in Texas who had been fighting the Mexican government issued a Declaration of Independence. Four days later, they were defeated in the Battle of the Alamo, which became a symbol of American courage and heroic endeavour. In April, the Mexican army lost decisively to Sam Houston's forces at the Battle of San Jacinto, and Texas became a republic. Its admittance to the Union in 1845 helped to provoke the war between the United States and Mexico, which broke out a year later.

issue in his 1832 campaign and his action gained him widespread support.

On 28 February 1827, the Baltimore and Ohio Railroad, running from Maryland across Virginia to the Ohio River, received its charter. The first US railroad had opened the previous year in John Adams's home town of Quincy, but the Baltimore and Ohio would enable passengers to travel from east to west. In 1833, Andrew Jackson became the first president to travel on one of its steam trains.

BATTLE WITH THE BANK

Jackson's battle with the National Bank continued. When his treasury secretary refused to switch federal government deposits to state banks, the president sacked him. His replacement, the attorney general Roger B. Taney, was not confirmed by the Senate, which, led by Calhoun and Clay, passed a motion of censure against Jackson. The president was not deterred.

In 1835, on the death of John Marshall, Jackson became the first president since John Adams in 1801 to appoint a chief justice of the Supreme Court. His choice was Taney, whose nomination again caused controversy, but who was eventually confirmed by the Senate. Taney, from Maryland, south

of the Mason–Dixon line, would have a major influence in shaping the Court's decisions during the next 30 years.

RETIREMENT

Jackson lived at the Hermitage for his last eight years, remaining involved in Democrat party politics. In 1844 he was instrumental in its nomination of James

Above: Jackson's meeting with the Native American leader Red Eagle.

Polk, known as 'Young Hickory', as its presidential candidate. Andrew Jackson, a leading actor in the developing drama of presidential politics during his lifetime, died peacefully, aged 78, on 8 June 1845.

STATES ENTERING THE UNION DURING JACKSON'S PRESIDENCY:

ARKANSAS

Entered the Union: 15 June 1836
Pre-state history: Part of Missouri Territory, organized as Arkansas Territory (1819)
Total population in 1840 census: 97,574
Total number of slaves in 1840 census: 19,935
Electoral College votes in 1836: 3

MICHIGAN

Entered the Union: 26 January 1837
Pre-state history: Acquired by British (1763); ceded to US (1783); part of Northwest Territory (1787); organized as Michigan Territory (1805)
Total population in 1840 census: 212,267
Total number of slaves in 1840 census: 0
Electoral College votes in 1836: 3
(Michigan entered the union nine days before the electoral college met.)

THE REVOLT AGAINST SLAVERY

1831

In his farewell address in 1837, Andrew Jackson drew attention to what he called "systematic efforts publicly made to sow the seeds of discord between different parts of the United States, and to place party divisions directly upon geographical distinctions; to excite the South against the North, and the North against the South, and to force into the controversy the most delicate and exciting topics upon which it is impossible that a large portion of the Union can ever speak without strong emotions". He was referring to slavery and abolitionism, which, during his presidency, had become the two

Below: Turner's rebellion, which he believed was directed by God, was one of the bloodiest in American history.

Left: The Liberator advocated an immediate end to slavery.

political poles that increasingly threatened to tear the United States apart.

Unlike his predecessors, Jackson did not agonize over the morality of slavery but he did appreciate clearly its destructive potential. He had seen in the nullification crisis in South Carolina an example of the serious consequences of a slave-holding state's refusal to accept the legitimacy of the federal government's laws. He had also witnessed the growth of the abolitionist movement in the North.

In the year Jackson left office, the federal Constitution was 50 years old but the problem that had been present from the beginnings of the American republic had still not been resolved. It had been dramatized during his presidency by the agitations of an abolitionist, William Lloyd Garrison, and the actions of a slave, Nat Turner, who led a rebellion in Virginia.

WILLIAM LLOYD GARRISON

In January 1831, in the inaugural editorial of *The Liberator*, William Lloyd Garrison, the newspaper's editor, announced that during a tour of New England, speaking out against slavery, he had: "determined, at every hazard, to lift up the standard of emancipation in the eyes of the nation, within sight of Bunker Hill and in the birthplace of liberty". The weekly newspaper he was driven to publish would appear continuously for the next 35 years.

Garrison was born in Massachusetts in 1805. In the 1820s he joined the American Colonization Society, which, with the support of President Monroe, worked to establish Liberia on the coast of West Africa as a place of repatriation for former slaves. However, Garrison became disillusioned with the society's policy of helping those already free rather than attacking the institution of slavery itself. After he had founded *The Liberator* he joined other abolitionists in establishing pressure groups dedicated to the cause, including, in 1833, the American Anti-Slavery Society.

NAT TURNER'S REBELLION

While Garrison was becoming an increasingly vociferous advocate for abolitionism, Nat Turner, an intelligent and deeply religious slave in Virginia, took matters into his own hands. In August 1831, Turner's spontaneous uprising began with a handful of his followers and turned into the South's nightmare: a rebellion in which more than 80 slaves joined in a killing spree, indiscriminately attacking white families until the state militia regained control of the situation. For Garrison, writing in *The Liberator* the following month: "What was poetry, imagination, in January, is now a bloody reality."

Right: The American Anti-Slavery Society had become a national organization by 1840. It was supported by religious groups and free black people, and soon became a platform for women to speak in public.

After a perfunctory trial, Turner was found guilty of murdering 55 white men, women and children. He had, he confessed, been motivated by mystical visions and had seen "white spirits and black spirits in battle, and the sun was darkened, the thunder rolled in the heavens, and blood flowed in streams".

Abolitionists and slave owners reacted to the revolt in predictable ways. For Garrison it was a vindication of his argument that the continuation of slavery would lead inevitably to violence. The South's only hope was the immediate emancipation of its slaves. On the other hand, John Floyd, then governor of Virginia, had no doubt what had caused the uprising: "The spirit of insubordination … had its origin among, and emanated from, the Yankee population." Floyd blamed the abolitionists for their "incendiary publications" – such as *The Liberator* – which were encouraging the slaves to rebel, and he proposed stringent measures in an attempt to prevent any further such incidents.

Turner's revolt occurred while Alexis de Tocqueville, one of the most famous commentators on 19th-century American politics, society and culture,

ALEXIS DE TOCQUEVILLE

French aristocrat, Alexis de Tocqueville (1805–59), embarked on an 18-month tour of the United States in 1831. His analysis of its class structure and the importance of the work ethic, with other perceptive observations on US politics, society and culture, were published in two volumes under the title *Democracy in America* (1835 and 1840). His work soon became established as the most famous and influential 19th-century study of the United States.

was visiting the United States from France. After touring the South, he had been left in no doubt about the future of its 'peculiar institution', predicting that, "If liberty be refused to the Negroes of the South, they will in the end forcibly seize it for themselves."

De Tocqueville was wrong in one vital respect. It would take a civil war between the white populations of the North and the South, and a proclamation by one of America's greatest presidents, Abraham Lincoln, to bring the slaves their freedom.

INDIAN REMOVAL
THE 'TRAIL OF TEARS'

In his first inaugural address, Andrew Jackson proclaimed: "It will be my sincere and constant desire to observe toward the Indian tribes within our limits a just and liberal policy, and to give that humane and considerate attention to their rights and their wants which is consistent with the habits of our Government and the feelings of our people." His rhetoric did not match reality. He had fought against Native Americans as a military commander. As president he displaced them from their ancestral lands.

NATIVE DISPLACEMENT

Following the Indian Removal Act of 1830, some tribes, the Choctaws and the Chickasaws among them, signed treaties with the federal government and moved west, reluctantly and only after white settlers had occupied their lands.

At the end of Jackson's administration, in 1837, the Seminole Indians went to war rather than leave. Their struggle lasted seven costly years.

No treaty was signed with the Creeks living in Alabama. The secretary of war, Lewis Cass, sent General Winfield Scott to force them off their land. After the Senate ratified the Treaty of New Echota, which agreed terms for American Indian removal in 1836, the Cherokee had two years to move west voluntarily, but only 2,000 members of the tribe complied. In 1838, Winfield Scott arrived in Georgia. Sixteen thousand Cherokee were rounded up by his troops, and forced to move west from their homelands there as well as from Tennessee, Alabama and North Carolina. Four thousand died on the 'Trail of Tears', the most visible symbol of the impact of this forced migration

of Native American tribes westwards to land that later became part of Oklahoma. By the time he left office, Jackson's policy had resulted in the removal of most members of the five major tribes inhabiting the south-east of the United States to territory beyond the Mississippi River.

Alexis de Tocqueville observed that the United States was able "to exterminate the Indian race ... without violating a single great principle of morality in the eyes of the world". Whereas the reaction against slavery inspired the abolitionist movement, action against Native Americans proceeded with only the occasional objection to its legality, and no sustained condemnation of its immorality.

Below: With the settler population burgeoning, native tribes were stripped of their land.

MARTIN VAN BUREN

1837–1841

It should have been the crowning achievement of a long political career, but as president, Martin Van Buren found difficulty in escaping from Andrew Jackson's long shadow. At his inauguration, as Thomas Hart Benton put it, "For once, the rising was eclipsed by the setting sun."

Van Buren was born in New York in 1782 and was the son of immigrants from Holland. In 1803, he qualified as a lawyer and four years later he married Hannah Hoes, who was also of Dutch descent. They had four children.

In 1812 Van Buren became a state senator and by 1820 he was leader of the 'Albany Regency', the power-brokers in New York's capital city who controlled state politics. The following year he entered the Senate in Washington. After 1824, as a leading opponent of John Quincy Adams, Van Buren organized the Democrats behind Jackson's candidacy. He served as secretary of state and vice president.

To gain Southern support during the 1836 election campaign, Van Buren made it clear that he tolerated slavery where it existed, and was against the abolitionists' campaign to prohibit it in Washington DC. On the other hand, he was opposed to the annexation of Texas if it was to bring with it a further extension of slavery. Successive presidential candidates had to walk a political tightrope between the pressures of expansion and the mounting opposition to slavery, and Van Buren was no exception. Winning the 1836 election as Jackson's chosen successor, he was the third widower to enter the White House: in 1819 his wife had died from tuberculosis at the age of 35.

Above: Van Buren's presidency was defined by the poverty of the era in which he occupied the White House.

ADMINISTRATION

In his inaugural address Van Buren graciously praised his "illustrious predecessor", but the economic problems that Van Buren faced in his own presidential term were in part of Jackson's making. Jackson had encouraged demand for hard currency, gold and silver. In 1837 America's banks could no longer exchange paper money for the precious metals. The resulting financial panic soon became a full-blown economic depression, with a predictable impact on Van Buren's political popularity.

Conscious of potential divisions among Democrats and between North and South, Van Buren did his best not to inflame the increasingly bitter argument over slavery. His level-headed refusal to bow to agitation for the annexation of Texas by the United States avoided war with Mexico but also lost him popular support. In 1840, he failed to gain re-election.

RETIREMENT

Van Buren professed that the two happiest days of his life were the one on which he became president and the one on which he left the White House. This did not stop him trying to regain the presidency in 1844 and in 1848. For the remainder of his life he lived near Kinderhook, the village in which he had been born. He died in 1862, having seen his greatest fear, civil war, become a catastrophic reality.

Born: 5 December 1782, Kinderhook, New York
Parents: Abraham (1737–1817) and Maria (1748–1817)
Family background: Farming and tavern keeping
Education: Kinderhook Academy (1796)
Religion: Dutch Reformed
Occupation: Lawyer
Slave owner: Yes – but not while president
Political career: New York State senator, 1813–15
New York attorney general, 1815–19
United States Senate, 1821–9
Governor of New York, 1829
Secretary of state, 1829–31
Minister to England, 1831
Vice president, 1833–7
Presidential annual salary: $25,000
Political party: Democrat
Died: 24 July 1862, Kinderhook

HANNAH VAN BUREN

Hannah Hoes was born in 1783 in the same town as her cousin, Martin Van Buren, and her first language, like his, was Dutch. They married in 1807 and had four sons who survived to adulthood. Hannah died in 1817 and Van Buren did not re-marry. While president, he invited his daughter-in-law, Angelica Singleton, to act as his official White House hostess.

WILLIAM HENRY HARRISON
1841

The third former general to become commander-in-chief, following his second campaign for the White House, William Henry Harrison was the first president to die in office. He was born in Virginia in 1773 into a well-off family: his parents were friends of George and Martha Washington, and his father served three times as state governor. He entered the military in 1791, spending four years battling Native Americans in the Ohio Territory and taking command of Fort Washington near Cincinnati, which was founded by his future father-in-law.

In 1800, President John Adams appointed William Harrison to be governor of the Indiana Territory, a post in which he remained for 12 years. In 1811, he led the military expedition against Tecumseh's Native American

Born: 9 February 1773, Berkeley, Virginia

Parents: Benjamin (1726–91) and Elizabeth (1730–92)

Family background: Plantation owners, politics

Education: Hampden-Sydney College, near Richmond, Virginia

Religion: Episcopalian

Occupation: Soldier

Slave owner: Yes – but not while president

Political career: Secretary of Northwest Territory, 1798

Territorial delegate to Congress, 1799–1801

Territorial governor of Indiana, 1801–13

US Congressman from Ohio, 1816–19

United States senator, 1825–8

Minister to Colombia, 1828–9

Presidential annual salary: $25,000

Political party: Whig

Died: 4 April 1841, Washington DC

confederation and emerged victorious from the battle that would earn him his nickname: 'Old Tippecanoe'. Further success in the War of 1812 enhanced his military reputation, but his political career spluttered along.

THE FIRST WHIG PRESIDENT

Although John Quincy Adams objected to Harrison's "rabid taste for lucrative public office", he appointed him ambassador to Colombia, where he remained for a year. In 1829 Andrew Jackson, an old political enemy, recalled him. Harrison retired to Ohio, where he became involved with the Whig opposition, and in 1836 campaigned unsuccessfully for the White House as one of three Whig candidates. Four years later, he defeated Van Buren to become the Whigs' first president.

Harrison had just celebrated his 68th birthday when he made his fatal mistake. On 4 March 1841, he delivered

Above: Harrison gave the longest inaugural address on record, but his presidency was the shortest in American history.

the longest inaugural speech in presidential history. He spoke for almost two hours, coatless and hatless on a cold wet Washington day. He pledged not to serve a second term and ended by taking "an affectionate leave" of his audience. He did just that: a month later he died from pneumonia.

ANNE HARRISON

Anne Symmes was born in 1775 and married Harrison in 1795. They had ten children, of whom four survived to see him become president. Anne did not accompany her husband to his inauguration, and was about to join him when he died. She lived on for 23 more years, dying in 1864 aged 88.

JOHN TYLER
1841–1845

The first president to inherit the office rather than be elected to it, John Tyler asserted what he claimed was his constitutional right of succession and took the oath of office two days after William Henry Harrison's death. He was a lawyer and an experienced politician, and knew the value of establishing a precedent. His action stopped speculation that he would be a caretaker chief executive but he was still regarded as the 'Accidental President'.

Born in 1790, he came, like his predecessor, from an affluent Virginia family: Tyler graduated from William and Mary College and embarked on a legal career. In 1811 he took his seat in Virginia's House of Delegates. For the following quarter of a century, with the exception of one year – 1822 – he served variously in the federal House of Representatives, the State Legislature,

Above: Tyler's father was a governor of the state and a friend of Thomas Jefferson.

like his father as governor, and in the federal Senate. A slave-owner and ardent supporter of states' rights, Tyler was fiercely critical of Andrew Jackson. In both 1836 and 1840 he was a Whig candidate for the vice presidency, campaigning as William Henry Harrison's running mate under the slogan 'Tippecanoe and Tyler Too'.

PRESIDENT WITHOUT SUPPORT
When he became president on Harrison's death he lacked an electoral mandate and his political relationships were turbulent. His opponents consistently referred to him as 'the acting president' and he was not taken seriously. When, for the second time, he vetoed a congressional bill re-establishing a National Bank, all but one of his Cabinet, which he had kept intact after Harrison's death, resigned.

His party rejected him. Seeking a populist issue to rally support, Tyler seized on Texas. He advocated its annexation but it did not save his political career. In 1844 Henry Clay became the Whigs' presidential candidate, and Tyler,

bowing to pressure – ironically from, among others, Andrew Jackson – withdrew from the contest.

He retired to Virginia. In 1861, following the South's secession, he was elected to the Confederate States Congress, but died the following year just prior to its first meeting.

Born: 29 March 1790, Greenway, Virginia
Parents: John (1747–1813) and Mary (1761–97)
Family background: Law, politics
Education: William and Mary College (1807)
Religion: Episcopalian
Occupation: Lawyer
Slave owner: Yes
Political career: Virginia House of Delegates, 1811–16
US House of Representatives, 1816–21
Virginia State Legislature, 1823–5
Governor of Virginia, 1825–6
US Senate, 1827–36
Vice president, 1841
Confederate States Congress, 1861–2
Presidential annual salary: $25,000
Political party: Whig
Died: 18 January 1862, Richmond, Virginia

STATES ENTERING THE UNION DURING TYLER'S PRESIDENCY: FLORIDA

Entered the Union: 3 March 1845
Pre-state history: Alternating Spanish and British control until acquired for US by Andrew Jackson (1821) and organized as Florida Territory (1822)
Total population in 1840 census: 54,477
Total number of slaves in 1840 census: 25,717
Electoral College votes in 1848: 3

LETITIA AND JULIA TYLER
Born in 1790, Letitia Christian married John Tyler in 1813. In 1842, she was the first president's wife to die in the White House, six months after she moved in. Two years later Tyler married Julia Gardiner, who was born in 1830. She died in 1889. Tyler had a total of 15 children, eight by Letitia and seven by Julia.

JAMES POLK
1845–1849

James Polk became president with the support of those Americans who were anxious to incorporate Texas into the United States. By the time he left office in 1849 he had acquired Oregon from the British and fought a war with Mexico that resulted in the United States gaining territories that would become seven new states in the West. Although it appeared to be the fulfilment of the United States' 'Manifest Destiny' to expand across the North American continent, these new lands once again focused attention on the fundamental fault line of slavery: the issue that, 12 years later, would plunge the nation into civil war.

Polk was born in North Carolina in 1795, but, like Andrew Jackson, his political life began in Tennessee. When he was 10, Polk's family moved there and prospered, building a plantation and owning slaves. He returned to North

Above: During Polk's presidency, the United States expanded westwards. The prospect of the extension of slavery into this new territory by including new states in the union agitated abolitionists.

Born: 2 November 1795, Mecklenburg County, North Carolina
Parents: Samuel (1772–1827) and Jane (1776–1852)
Family background: Farming
Education: University of North Carolina (1818)
Religion: Presbyterian
Occupation: Lawyer
Slave owner: Yes
Political career: Tennessee House of Representatives, 1823–5
US House of Representatives, 1825–39
Speaker of the House, 1835–9
Governor of Tennessee, 1839–41
Presidential annual salary: $25,000
Political party: Democrat
Died: 15 June 1849, Nashville, Tennessee

STATES ENTERING THE UNION DURING POLK'S PRESIDENCY:

TEXAS

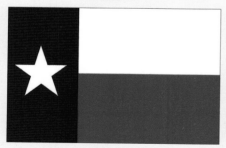

Entered the Union: 29 December 1845
Pre-state history: Claimed by Mexico following War of Independence against Spain (1821); proclaimed Independent Republic (1836); annexed by US (1845)
Total population in 1850 census: 212,592
Total number of slaves in 1850 census: 58,161
Electoral College votes in 1848: 4

IOWA

Entered the Union: 28 December 1846
Pre-state history: Part of Louisiana Purchase (1803); organized as Iowa Territory (1838)
Total population in 1850 census: 192,214
Total number of slaves in 1850 census: 0
Electoral College votes in 1848: 4

WISCONSIN

Entered the Union: 29 May 1848
Pre-state history: Acquired by British (1763); ceded to US (1783); part of Northwest Territory (1787); organized as Wisconsin Territory (1836)
Total population in 1850 census: 305,391
Total number of slaves in 1850 census: 0
Electoral College votes in 1848: 4

MANIFEST DESTINY

In July 1845, the journalist John L. O'Sullivan wrote an article in the *United States Magazine and Democratic Review* supporting the annexation of Texas. He argued that it was the United States' "manifest destiny to overspread the continent allotted by providence for the free development of our yearly multiplying millions". His phrase – "manifest destiny" – was subsequently widely used as a justification of the continued expansion of the United States across the North American continent.

Left: Columbia, the personification of the United States, is seen leading settlers in a westward expansion, while the native people flee.

Carolina to attend university, graduating in 1818. After studying law in Nashville, in 1823 he entered the Tennessee House of Representatives.

Polk was first elected to the federal House of Representatives in 1825, and served there for 14 years. With Jackson's support, in 1835 he became its Speaker. His endorsement of President Jackson's policies earned him his nickname, 'Young Hickory'. In 1839 he returned to Tennessee and served one term as state governor.

THE 1844 ELECTION

The major issue in the 1844 election was whether the independent republic of Texas, a slave-owning region, should be annexed – in other words added – to the Union as a slave state. Polk, again helped by Jackson's endorsement, became the party's compromise candidate. The Whigs chose Henry Clay, who, like Van Buren, was against annexation. Initially Tyler, who had been denied the Whig nomination, was

Right: Canada and the United States both claimed the right to Oregon in the north-west of America.

convinced that by incorporating Texas in the Union he could win the election in his own right, without needing the support of a party organization. Instead he was persuaded that his candidacy would split the pro-Texas vote and benefit Clay. He stepped aside, allowing a straight fight between the two major parties. Polk won by a narrow margin. Just before he left the White House,

Tyler, acting on a joint congressional resolution, offered Texas the prospect of admission to the Union before 1 January 1846.

TEXAS

After Texas joined the Union in December 1845, fighting broke out with Mexico, which had never recognized the new state's claim to be an

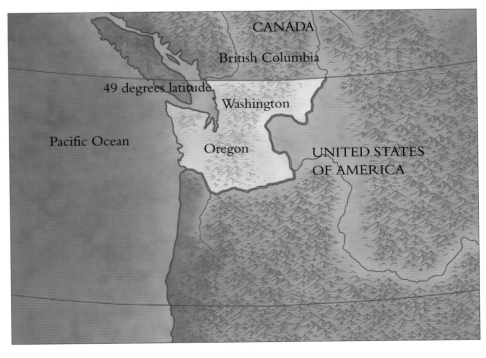

Left: The star among the stripes indicates Polk's support of the admission of Texas.

independent republic. In May 1846 Polk asked Congress for a Declaration of War, claiming that Mexican troops had attacked and killed US soldiers stationed on the Texas border under the command of General Zachary Taylor: "American blood had been shed on American soil." Not everyone was convinced by the president's argument. One member of the Whig party in Congress disputed whether the incident had indeed occurred on United States territory: his name was Abraham Lincoln. Congress nevertheless supported the president. Although there were some who opposed the United States' action – Henry David Thoreau became a famous protester – within two years, after a number of military setbacks, Mexico had admitted defeat.

Below: The gold rush quickly changed the balance of state populations but few became rich and many endured harsh conditions.

OREGON

Both Britain and the United States had territorial interests in the Oregon Country in the north-west, and the boundary had been the subject of dispute for several decades. Polk now hoped to admit Oregon as a free state, balancing the slave state of Texas. To gain the support of American expansionists, he had campaigned on the slogan 'Fifty-four Forty or Fight', calling for the entire territory up to the latitude of 54° 40' north to be claimed by the United States. But faced with the prospect of conducting two simultaneous wars (with Britain and Mexico) in June 1846, Polk compromised. A treaty was concluded with Britain, establishing America's north-west border with Canada along the 49th parallel. The United States gained what would become the states of Oregon, Montana, Washington and Idaho.

POPULATION BOOM

Iowa entered the Union in 1846, followed two years later by Wisconsin, both as free states. As its territory increased, so did America's attraction to European immigrants. During Polk's

presidency, the Irish potato famine encouraged many to seek a new life across the Atlantic. Settlers swarmed over the continent.

In January 1848, gold was discovered in California, and the territory's population grew rapidly as a result of the rush to find more. As it applied for statehood, the need to resolve the controversy over whether slavery should be permitted to extend to the West became more pressing.

By then, Polk was no longer president. His health had deteriorated throughout his time in office. In 1848 he kept his promise not to seek re-election. The Whigs, many of whom had opposed the Mexican War, were its major beneficiaries. Their candidate, Zachary Taylor, won the election. In June 1849, less than four months after he had left the White House, Polk died.

WAR WITH MEXICO
1846–1848

Following America's declaration of war on Mexico in May 1846, General Zachary Taylor's US forces invaded. Although outnumbered by the Mexican army, the Americans won the Battle of Palo Alto, and by September Taylor had taken the city of Monterrey in northern Mexico. By that time another US army, commanded by General Stephen Watts Kearny, had occupied Santa Fe, in the region that would later become the American state of New Mexico. Kearny then led some of his troops into California to link up with forces under Captain John Fremont. Others fought their way into Mexican territory and through Chihuahua to meet with Taylor's army in spring 1847.

Meanwhile, the former Mexican president, Santa Anna, saw an opportunity to revive his turbulent political career. He returned from Cuba, where he had lived in exile following a coup in 1844. In return for a guarantee of safe passage, he had assured Polk that once restored to power he would negotiate a peace favourable to the Americans in return for $30 million. He was bluffing. After regaining the presidency, he marched north from Mexico City with an 18,000-strong army to confront Taylor. On 22 February 1847, despite being once again heavily outnumbered, the Americans beat Santa Anna's forces at the Battle of Buena Vista.

The following month General Winfield Scott embarked on an ambitious expedition by sea and land, capturing the port of Veracruz in March and then fighting a six-month campaign, at the end of which he captured Mexico City. Santa Anna was deposed again and the new Mexican government surrendered. Under the terms of the Treaty of Guadeloupe, signed on 2 February 1848, Mexico ceded half its territory to the United States, agreeing to $15 million compensation for the loss of California and New Mexico and the establishment of the border along the Rio Grande.

It was a one-sided war. About 700 Americans died in battle, although 18 times that number succumbed to

Above: The Battle of Palo Alto was the first battle of the Mexican War: the United States won all the major engagements between the two sides.

disease. Mexico suffered almost 50,000 casualties. Of the US commanders and troops who took part, many would later find themselves on opposite sides during the Civil War.

Below: The war with Mexico was controversial in Congress, but its hero Zachary Taylor became America's next president.

CHAPTER FOUR

ZACHARY TAYLOR TO ANDREW JOHNSON
1849–1869

THE 20 YEARS BETWEEN 1849 AND 1869 BEGAN WITH THE ISSUE OF SLAVERY STILL DOMINATING AMERICAN POLITICS, CULMINATED IN THE CIVIL WAR, AND ENDED WITH A PRESIDENT ASSASSINATED AND HIS SUCCESSOR ESCAPING IMPEACHMENT BY A SINGLE VOTE. TWO WHIGS, TWO DEMOCRATS, THE FIRST REPUBLICAN PRESIDENT AND A SOUTHERN DEMOCRAT WHO HAD REMAINED LOYAL TO THE UNION WOULD OCCUPY THE WHITE HOUSE DURING TWO OF THE MOST DRAMATIC DECADES IN AMERICAN HISTORY. AS ABOLITIONISTS ARGUED FOR AN END TO SLAVERY, IN 1848 A CONVENTION, MEETING AT SENECA FALLS, NEW YORK, HAD ISSUED ITS 'DECLARATION OF SENTIMENTS', A DEFINING MOMENT IN THE LONG STRUGGLE FOR WOMEN'S EQUALITY. THE ELECTION OF ABRAHAM LINCOLN IN 1860 HASTENED THE SOUTH'S SECESSION AND THE OUTBREAK OF THE CIVIL WAR BUT BROUGHT TO THE WHITE HOUSE ONE OF AMERICA'S GREATEST PRESIDENTS.

Left: The Battle of Gettysburg, the turning point of the Civil War, saw the largest number of casualties.

ZACHARY TAYLOR
1849–1850

The fourth military hero to become president, Zachary Taylor's affiliation to the Whigs owed more to the party's desire to win back the White House than to his ideological convictions. Taylor tried to remain 'above politics', cultivating the image of an outsider and grazing his favourite old army horse, 'Whitey', on the White House lawn.

Taylor's father had been an aide to George Washington during the War of Independence. Taylor grew up in Kentucky on what became a prosperous plantation. He joined the military and by 1808 he was a lieutenant. He served under William Henry Harrison. Taylor briefly resigned his commission in 1815, but rejoined the army the following year and lived the peripatetic life of an army officer while his career steadily advanced. After his exploits during the Mexican War, he became a popular choice for the presidency in 1848. His defeat of the Democrat candidate, Lewis Cass, was helped, ironically, by the intervention of the Free Soil Party, a coalition of his opponents. Their candidate, the former president Martin Van Buren, split the Democrats' support, particularly in New York, delivering Taylor the White House by a margin of 36 electoral college votes.

THE ISSUE OF SLAVERY

As president, Zachary Taylor, who was a slave owner, had to confront the intractable problem that his success as a soldier had helped create: should slavery be extended west into the territories acquired as a result of the Mexican War? He disappointed Southerners, and advocated the entry of California and New Mexico into the Union as free states. When Southern leaders talked of secession, he threatened to hang those who conspired against the Union.

Extremism on both sides encouraged politicians to seek what little common ground remained. A compromise was being debated in the Senate when, on 4 July 1850, the president attended a ceremony at the still incomplete Washington Monument. He fell ill after consuming copious amounts of fruit, cold milk and iced water. Five days later, he died, after only 16 months in office.

Born: 24 November 1784, near Barboursville, Virginia
Parents: Richard (1744–1829) and Sarah (1760–1822)
Family background: Military, landowning
Education: Not formally educated
Religion: Episcopalian
Occupation: Soldier
Slave owner: Yes
Political career: No political office prior to presidency
Presidential annual salary: $25,000
Political party: Whig
Died: 9 July 1850, Washington DC

MARGARET TAYLOR

Born in Maryland in 1788, Margaret Smith married Zachary Taylor in 1810. The Taylors had six children. In 1820, two of them died of a fever that also affected their mother's health. Another daughter, Sarah, died shortly after marrying Jefferson Davis. In the White House Margaret avoided public functions. She died in Mississippi in 1852, aged 63.

Left: Taylor's military reputation helped the Whigs recapture the White House; as president his party allegiance was always weak.

THE COMPROMISE
1850

Victory in the Mexican War brought the United States more territory but focused attention once more on the problem of slavery. The Compromise of 1850 was Congress's attempt to provide a legislative framework in answer to a series of controversial questions. Should California be admitted as a free state, thereby disrupting the delicate balance of slave-owning and free states that had been the cornerstone of Clay's compromise 30 years earlier? Should Texas be allowed to claim more land from New Mexico? Should slavery be tolerated in the nation's capital?

Would more territory mean more slavery? This question was the divisive and decisive issue in government. The Compromise of 1850 represented the last great effort to hold the Union together. In the end it merely postponed what eight years later Senator William Seward from New York would call the "irrepressible conflict" between North and South. The complex negotiations involved politicians from both major

parties – Democrats and Whigs – who eventually worked their way to common ground. Once again the architect of the compromise was Henry Clay, who confronted several related problems.

THE COMPROMISE IS DEBATED

The Senate debate, which began in January, lasted nine months. The major protagonists were Clay, who was now 70, Stephen Douglas from Illinois, and, before he became Millard Fillmore's secretary of state, Daniel Webster from Massachusetts. Calhoun (a former vice president), who privately admitted that the South "cannot with safety remain in the Union … and there is little or no prospect of any change for the better", died aged 68 on 31 March, before a final agreement had been reached.

The Compromise postponed the decision as to whether slavery should be allowed in New Mexico, Nevada, Arizona and Utah. It was agreed that their inhabitants would resolve the issue after they had organized for statehood. In the event, none of these territories would reach the population thresholds

Above: Henry Clay was instrumental in putting together the Compromise of 1850, which delayed the crisis of secession for another decade.

that allowed them to enter the Union until after 1863, when Abraham Lincoln issued the Emancipation Proclamation signalling the end of slavery.

California was admitted as a free state. Texas gave up its territorial claims in return for $10 million. Slavery was still permitted in Washington DC, but the slave trade there – it was the largest market in the country – was ended.

The most controversial part of the agreement was the Fugitive Slave Act, passed to placate the South, which required that escaped slaves be returned to their owners. It enraged abolitionists. In 1852, one of them, Harriet Beecher Stowe, published *Uncle Tom's Cabin*, a searing indictment of slavery. Later, President Lincoln would acknowledge its impact in contributing to the popular mood that, despite the Compromise, would lead inexorably to the outbreak of the Civil War.

THE SENECA FALLS CONVENTION 1848

Around 300 people, including about 40 men, attended the first women's rights convention, which took place at Seneca Falls, New York, on 19 and 20 July 1848. Its principal organizers were Lucretia Mott and Elizabeth Cady Stanton. The meeting agreed the 'Declaration of Sentiments', written by Stanton and drawing its inspiration from the language used by Thomas Jefferson in 1776. The openness of American society had created opportunities for women to take up public roles, often as educators. Many of those involved in the struggle for women's rights were also active in the causes of abolitionism and temperance.

MILLARD FILLMORE
1850–1853

Millard Fillmore spent the first six months of 1850 presiding over the Senate as it debated the Compromise that it hoped might avoid the South's imminent secession. On 10 July 1850 he became the 13th president, following Zachary Taylor's death the previous night. He supported the Compromise of 1850, but his presidency imploded as political attitudes became polarized.

Born in 1800 in the frontier township of Locke, New York, Fillmore escaped a life of poverty through determined self-improvement, qualifying as a lawyer at the age of 23. He began his political career as a member of the single-issue Anti-Masonic party – which was gradually absorbed into the Whig party during the 1830s – in opposition to Andrew Jackson, who was a Mason. In 1843 he narrowly failed to become governor of New York; he was elected the state's financial comptroller in 1847, and the following year he was nominated as the vice-presidential candidate

Above: Fillmore replaced Taylor's Cabinet, with supporters of the 1850 Compromise.

for the Whigs, balancing the ticket headed by Taylor, whose home was then the slave state of Louisiana.

DEMISE OF THE WHIGS

Fillmore immediately restructured the Cabinet to include like-minded Whigs, including Daniel Webster who became secretary of state. In September 1850 he signed the Compromise measures into law, including the controversial Fugitive Slave Act, which, despite his anti-slavery sentiments, he felt he had the constitutional duty to enforce. His gesture boosted the activities of the Underground Railroad, which helped escaped slaves move north, and also stirred up abolitionist sentiment. This deepened political division within the Whig party, and in 1852, hopelessly disunited, they preferred to nominate another general, Winfield Scott, as their candidate. Fillmore would be the party's last president.

Fillmore was the second vice president to inherit the presidency, and like John Tyler he never won election to the White House. He was once again

STATES ENTERING THE UNION DURING FILLMORE'S PRESIDENCY: CALIFORNIA

Entered the Union: 9 September 1850

Pre-state history: Claimed by Mexico following War of Independence against Spain (1821); proclaimed Independent Republic for one week during Mexican–American War (1846); ceded to US (1848)

Total population in 1850 census: 92,597

Total number of slaves in 1850 census: 0

Electoral College votes in 1852: 4

attracted to the political fringe. In 1856, he became the presidential candidate of the strongly anti-immigrant and strangely named 'Know Nothing' party, winning only Maryland's eight electoral college votes. He died in 1874.

Born: 7 January 1800, Locke Township (now Summerhill), New York
Parents: Nathaniel (1771–1863) and Phoebe (1780–1831)
Family background: Farming
Education: Not formally educated
Religion: Unitarian
Occupation: Lawyer
Slave owner: No
Political career: New York State Assembly, 1828–31
US House of Representatives, 1833–5, 1837–45
Comptroller of New York, 1847
Vice president, 1849–50
Presidential annual salary: $25,000
Political party: Whig
Died: 8 March 1874, Buffalo, New York

ABIGAIL FILLMORE

Abigail Powers was born in 1798 in New York. She married in 1826 and had two children, a son named for his father, and a daughter called Mary. She founded the White House library. In 1842, an accident caused her health to deteriorate; she died of pneumonia in 1853, shortly after attending Franklin Pierce's inauguration. Her death was followed a year later by that of Mary.

FRANKLIN PIERCE
1853–1857

Franklin Pierce's family traced its ancestry to the Puritans. After graduation at the age of 20, he embarked on a career that mixed the law, politics, alcohol (he was a heavy drinker) and the military. He entered the New Hampshire State Legislature in 1829. Four years later he was elected to Congress, returning home in 1842 to practise law. Pierce volunteered for military service during the Mexican War of 1848, and at its end resumed his political career to become leader of New Hampshire's Democrat party. In the 1852 presidential election he defeated his former commanding officer, General Winfield Scott.

Between his election and inauguration, Pierce and his wife were involved in an accident which killed their son. The tragedy cast a cloud over their relationship and his presidency.

INEFFECTIVE GOVERNMENT
The first Northern Democrat since Martin Van Buren to win the White House, Franklin Pierce's four years in office were marked by increasing conflict between pro-slavery and anti-slavery forces. In Kansas, civil war broke out over the issue.

JANE PIERCE
Jane Appleton was born in New Hampshire in 1806 and married Pierce in 1834. Unlike her husband she believed in both temperance and abolitionism, and he periodically moderated his affection for liquor in respect of her commitment to the temperance movement. They had three sons, and the death of her youngest and only surviving boy just before she entered the White House plunged her into depression. She died in Massachusetts in 1863.

Above: Pierce was widely regarded as a 'doughface', a Northerner who tolerated slavery in the South. Democrats refused to nominate him for a second term.

In his inaugural address Pierce made his beliefs clear: "That the laws of 1850, commonly called the 'compromise measures', are strictly constitutional; and to be unhesitatingly carried into effect." To his critics, he was a 'doughface' – a Northerner with Southern sympathies.

Within six months of the Gadsden Purchase in 1853, Congress passed the Kansas–Nebraska Act, so that a northern railroad could be built from Chicago to the west coast. This repealed the Missouri Compromise, organizing these territories for statehood under the principle of 'popular sovereignty' and leaving the question of slavery to the inhabitants to decide. The battle lines crystallized. A guerrilla war broke out between pro- and anti-slavery settlers in the territory of Kansas – known as 'Bleeding Kansas' – over the question of whether it would enter the Union as a free or a slave state.

With the Whigs in terminal decline as an electoral force, the Democrats now faced opposition from the Republicans, a party formed from abolitionist Northerners who had opposed the

GADSDEN PURCHASE
With the aim of acquiring land south of the mountains to facilitate the building of a southern transcontinental railroad, James Gadsden was sent to Mexico by President Pierce to negotiate the purchase of an area of about 75,000 sq km (30,000 sq miles) in what is now southern Arizona and New Mexico. The treaty was signed in Mexico in 1853, agreeing a price of $10 million, but aroused controversy because abolitionists saw it as a way of expanding slave territory in the South.

repeal of the Missouri Compromise. Pierce lost his own party's confidence over his support of the Kansas–Nebraska Act and became the first elected incumbent not to be re-nominated by his party. Instead the 1856 Democrat convention nominated James Buchanan. Pierce retired into obscurity and died, all but forgotten, in 1869.

Born: 23 November 1804, Hillsborough (now Hillsboro), New Hampshire
Parents: Benjamin (1757–1839) and Elizabeth (1768–1844)
Family background: Military, farming, politics
Education: Bowdoin College (1824)
Religion: Episcopalian
Occupation: Lawyer, public official
Slave owner: No
Political career: New Hampshire Legislature, 1829–33
US House of Representatives, 1833–7
United States Senate, 1837–42
Presidential annual salary: $25,000
Political party: Democrat
Died: 8 October 1869, Concord, New Hampshire

JAMES BUCHANAN
1857–1861

By the time James Buchanan left the White House through the revolving door of presidential politics (since Andrew Jackson, no chief executive had managed to serve two terms) the United States had begun to disintegrate and the Democrat party had fallen apart. The combustible mixture of Northern abolitionism, Southern slavery and Western expansion ignited the fuse of secession that exploded into civil war. Faced with the impossibility of reconciling sectional differences, Buchanan did little to postpone what he and many of his contemporaries considered inevitable: the break-up of the United States.

James Buchanan volunteered for military service during the War of 1812, but did not see action, and afterwards

Below: Buchanan, an experienced politician and diplomat, could do nothing to prevent the nation's headlong rush towards civil war.

pursued a successful legal and political career. In 1819, following rumours that he had been seen with another woman, his fiancée, Anne Coleman, whose father had opposed their engagement, ended their relationship. She died a few days later: suicide was suspected. A devastated Buchanan never married.

Seeking solace in politics, he won election to Congress as a Federalist, and spent 10 years from 1821 in the House of Representatives. After his party's final collapse, he supported the Democrats. In 1832, President Jackson sent him to Russia as the US representative. Two years later he returned, becoming a member of the Senate until 1845 when President Polk appointed him secretary of state.

Buchanan had hoped for his party's presidential nomination in 1844 and tried for it again in 1852, only to lose out to Franklin Pierce, who appointed him ambassador to Britain. This enabled him to remain aloof from the political arguments resulting from the Kansas–Nebraska Act, but he was implicated in a controversial plan to acquire Cuba in order to allow the Southern slave economy to expand into the Caribbean. This made him suspect among those opposed to slavery, but his main rivals for the Democrats' presidential nomination in 1856, Franklin Pierce and Stephen Douglas, aroused even greater antipathy, and Buchanan emerged as the party's compromise candidate.

In a three-way contest against the Republican John Fremont and the former president Millard Fillmore, Buchanan won a minority of the popular vote. His convincing majority in the electoral college was built on solid support from the slave-owning South: he carried only four Northern states. The new president of the United States had been elected by an incontestably divided nation. He realized

Born: 23 April 1791, Cove Gap (near Mercersburg), Pennsylvania
Parents: James (1761?–1821) and Elizabeth (1767–1833)
Family background: Store keeping
Education: Dickinson College (1809)
Religion: Presbyterian
Occupation: Lawyer
Slave owner: No
Political career: Pennsylvania House of Representatives, 1815–16
US House of Representatives, 1821–31
Minister to Russia, 1832–4
United States Senate, 1834–45
Secretary of state, 1845–9
Minister to Britain, 1853–6
Presidential annual salary: $25,000
Political party: Democrat
Died: 1 June 1868, Wheatland (near Lancaster), Pennsylvania

what was at stake, predicting before he was inaugurated that: "Before many years the abolitionists will bring war upon this land. It may come during the next presidential term." During his term the United States began to disintegrate.

ADMINISTRATION

In his inaugural address Buchanan announced that he would not seek a second term in office. Two days later, the Supreme Court announced its decision in the case of Dred Scott v. Sanford. Its

DRED SCOTT V. SANFORD

In 1857, in the case of Dred Scott v. Sanford, the Supreme Court decided that African-Americans had no rights of citizenship, that slavery should be permitted in the western territories, and that the Missouri Compromise of 1850 was unconstitutional.

Above: Buchanan with his Cabinet of 1859, many of whose members resigned on the secession of the Confederate states.

pro-slavery stance galvanized abolitionist sentiment. In December a rigged referendum in Kansas approved the Lecompton Constitution, which would have permitted slavery in the state.

In 1858, Buchanan reiterated the language of expansionism, telling Congress, "It is, beyond question, the destiny of our race to spread themselves over the continent of North America." He also had overseas ambitions. Throughout his administration he encouraged plans to annexe Cuba, intensifying Republican opposition and confirming their assessment that like his predecessor he was a 'doughface' who favoured the expansion of slavery.

In 1859, the Republicans won a majority in the House of Representatives, but the Senate and the president's veto blocked any anti-slavery legislation and led to a political stalemate. With the next presidential election looming, the militant abolitionist John Brown launched a quixotic raid on the federal armoury at Harper's Ferry in Virginia, hoping to use the captured munitions in the slave uprising he was convinced his action would provoke. This action further polarized opinion in the North and South.

Buchanan retired in 1861. While in office he did nothing to prevent the South's secession and the formation of a new Confederacy of slave-owning states. Blamed by his critics for the outbreak of the Civil War, he maintained that it was the fault of the Republicans and his successor, Lincoln. He supported the cause of the Union, and survived to see the end of the war.

STATES ENTERING THE UNION DURING BUCHANAN'S PRESIDENCY:

MINNESOTA	OREGON	KANSAS

Entered the Union: 11 May 1858
Pre-state history: Minnesota Territory organized from lands remaining from Iowa and Wisconsin Territories (1849)
Total population in 1860 census: 172,023
Total number of slaves in 1850 census: 0
Electoral College votes in 1860: 4

Entered the Union: 14 February 1859
Pre-state history: Border dispute with Britain resolved by treaty (1846); organized as Oregon Territory (1848)
Total population in 1860 census: 52,465
Total number of slaves in 1850 census: 0
Electoral College votes in 1860: 3

Entered the Union: 29 January 1861
Pre-state history: Part of Louisiana Purchase (1803); organized as Kansas Territory (1854)
Total population in 1860 census: 107,206
Total number of slaves in 1850 census: 2
Electoral College votes in 1864: 3

THE PRESIDENTIAL ELECTION
1860

There were two presidential elections in 1860: one in the North and one in the South. The Democrats, the only party that had previously commanded support across the nation, were by then hopelessly split, finding it impossible to settle on another compromise candidate like Pierce or Buchanan who could bridge the sectional divide.

During the turbulent 1850s, as the Western territories had organized for statehood, the basis of Democrat unity had been the principle of popular sovereignty advocated by their leader in the Senate, Stephen A. Douglas. This meant leaving it to the settlers to decide for themselves whether a new state would be for or against an extension of slavery. But by 1860, interpretations of the idea were so different as to cause a schism.

NORTH AND SOUTH

Northerners thought that popular sovereignty simply kept decision-making out of the hands of Washington politicians, and that in practical terms the

Below: The four candidates each drew on different sectional support as the nation finally fell apart.

Above: Lincoln and his running mate, Hannibal Hamlin from Maine, had no appeal below the Mason–Dixon line.

new territories would prove unsuitable for the extension of the slave economy. Southerners, meanwhile, stood by what they considered was their constitutional right to bring slaves into the territories. Only after slavery had made its presence felt there could a final choice be made as to whether it should continue after statehood was achieved. 'Bleeding Kansas' dramatized the issue, as pro-slavery and anti-slavery forces battled for territorial control and the violence illustrated the failure of the compromise.

REPUBLICANS AND DEMOCRATS

In April 1860, the Democrats held their national convention in Charleston, South Carolina. Southerners proposed that a federal slave code be adopted, guaranteeing the right to take slaves into the territories. When their idea was rejected, the Southern delegates walked out. Two months later, two separate Democrat conventions, both held in Baltimore, rallied behind different candidates. The Northerners nominated Stephen Douglas from Illinois. The group of breakaway Southerners fielded Buchanan's vice president, John Breckenridge from Kentucky.

The Republicans opposed the idea of popular sovereignty. While not all were committed to abolitionism – many

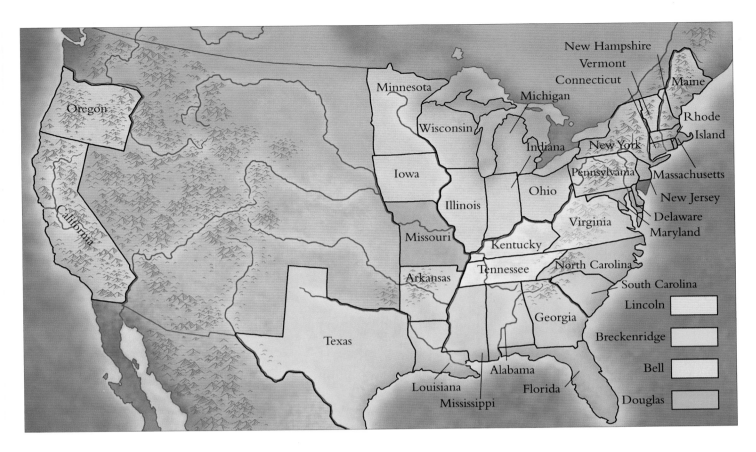

Map legend:
- Lincoln
- Breckenridge
- Bell
- Douglas

Republicans could tolerate the existing situation in the South – they nevertheless saw slavery as a moral rather than a political issue and were against its further expansion. The Republican party's candidate was Abraham Lincoln, whose electoral appeal was confined to the North.

The political landscape was further complicated by the new Constitutional Union party: a coalition of disaffected Whigs and the remnants of the Know Nothing party, hoping to appeal to those alienated by the acrimony of sectional politics. Lincoln's name did not appear on the ballot papers in most Southern states, where the Southern Democrat Breckenridge was opposed by the Constitutional Unionists' representative, John Bell, from Tennessee.

Of the 33 states then in the Union, 15 were slave-holding and 18 were free. Despite the South's over-representation in Congress and the electoral college, its electoral advantages were progressively unwinding as the North's population growth steadily outpaced it. By 1860 slave states had a total of 80 seats in the House of Representatives and 120 electoral college votes. Free states had 147 representatives in the House and 183 votes for the presidency.

With four candidates running for the White House in two distinct contests, the prospects of anyone gaining a majority of the popular vote were remote. Lincoln managed to gain around 40 per cent of it, without receiving a single vote in ten Southern states and only a small percentage in the remaining five slave states. Douglas received approximately 30 per cent, Breckenridge 18 per cent and Bell 12 per cent of the votes cast.

LINCOLN'S VICTORY

It was the electoral college that magnified the sectional divide. Lincoln's winning coalition was a result of his outright victory in 17 free states, which, together with the four additional votes he gained from New Hampshire, gave him a clear majority: 180 of the 303 electoral college votes cast. Douglas won Missouri, a slave state, and the support of the remaining three electors in New

Above: Lincoln's election in 1860 dramatized the division between free and slave states and led to the rapid secession of the South. The states that seceded from the union formed a confederacy of states and elected their own president.

Hampshire. In the deep South, Breckenridge captured 11 states, while Bell took only Kentucky and Virginia in addition to his home state of Tennessee. In Congress, the Republicans kept their majority in the House of Representatives. The Senate, in which only a third of the members could potentially be changed, stayed in the hands of the Democrats.

With the Democrats so clearly divided, the logic of the electoral mathematics was compelling: in the electoral college the South had become, as John Calhoun had predicted, "a fixed and helpless minority" and in the Congress its position was being steadily eroded. The 1860 election was not a mandate for abolitionism – far from it – but it encouraged the Southern states to consider their next step: secession.

ABRAHAM LINCOLN
1861–1865

Left: Shortly after Lincoln entered the White House, the Civil War broke out. A week after it ended, he was assassinated.

London summed him up: "He was hardly a representative Republican so much as a representative American."

BEGINNINGS

Abraham Lincoln was born in a log cabin in the slave state of Kentucky. His father, Thomas, was a farmer who moved his family to Indiana when Lincoln was seven. Two years later, his mother died. He had a difficult relationship with his functionally illiterate father, and in contrast it was his step-mother, Sarah Bush Johnston, who taught Lincoln the value of education and self-improvement, although his formal schooling was sporadic.

As a youth, he enjoyed life on the Mississippi, taking produce on a flatboat to sell in New Orleans. In 1830 his family moved to Illinois, and in the following year, after another river trip to Louisiana, Lincoln left home to live in New Salem, Illinois. He had been

In 1860, the election of Abraham Lincoln precipitated a constitutional crisis that was only resolved by war. Lincoln changed America. Even before his first inaugural address, seven Southern states had seceded and formed the Confederacy. During his first three months in office, they were joined by four others, and less than six weeks after he entered the White House, there was civil war. Lincoln fought the war initially on the pretext of forcing the South back into the Union, but in issuing the Emancipation Proclamation he acknowledged its ever-present subtext: the abolition of slavery.

Lincoln explored the limits of his presidential power, creating precedents that his successors would exploit for different purposes. During four years of conflict, his considerable political skills, inspirational rhetoric and ability to read the public mood rallied support for the Union cause. At Gettysburg, he would give one of America's most inspiring and enduring orations. In his moment of victory, he was assassinated. In its obituary pages, *The Times* newspaper of

STATES SECEDING FROM THE UNION

South Carolina	20 December 1860
Mississippi	9 January 1861
Florida	10 January 1861
Alabama	11 January 1861
Georgia	19 January 1861
Louisiana	26 January 1861
Texas	1 February 1861
Virginia	17 April 1861
Arkansas	6 May 1861
North Carolina	20 May 1861
Tennessee	8 June 1861

Born: 12 February 1809, Hardin (now Larue) County, Kentucky
Parents: Thomas (1778–1851) and Nancy (1784–1818)
Family background: Farming, wood-working
Education: Not formally educated
Religion: Not proclaimed
Occupation: Lawyer
Slave owner: No
Political career: Illinois State Legislature, 1834–42
US House of Representatives, 1847–9
Presidential annual salary: $25,000
Political party: Republican
Died: 15 April 1865, Washington DC

there only six months when he was encouraged to run for election to the state legislature. Lincoln's first campaign for state office was unsuccessful (he was to win a seat in 1834). During the election campaign he volunteered to fight in the Black Hawk War against local American Indians. He did not see action, but was elected captain of his local militia during the conflict in which Zachary Taylor, then a colonel in the regular army, also served.

By 1837 Lincoln had qualified as a lawyer, and he moved to a practice in Springfield, Illinois. In 1840 he

supported William Henry Harrison for president, and was selected as one of the Whig representatives in the electoral college when the party managed to elect its first successful candidate. Lincoln remained active in state politics, serving in the legislature until 1842.

As an Illinois Whig, Lincoln twice decided against running for governor in what was then a predominantly Democrat state. Instead he campaigned for a seat in the federal Congress, securing the nomination by pledging to serve only a single term. In 1846 he was elected to the House of Representatives. He vehemently opposed the conflict with Mexico in 1848, challenging President Polk to produce evidence of the provocation he had used as an excuse to demand a declaration of war.

Back in Illinois, Lincoln remained active in Whig politics but failed in an attempt to return to Washington as a senator. In 1856 he joined the new Republican party. At its convention in Philadelphia that year Lincoln's name was put forward as a vice-presidential candidate, but the nomination eventually went to William Dayton from New Jersey. Two years later he again ran for the Senate and his debates with his

opponent, the incumbent, Stephen Douglas, to whom he eventually lost, clarified the debate over slavery, and brought Lincoln national attention. By 1860 he was one of the leading contenders for the Republicans' presidential nomination, which he won at the party's convention in Chicago that May. Facing a weakened and divided Democrat opposition, Lincoln was elected president.

IMPENDING CRISIS

Lincoln's was not the only inaugural address that year. On 18 February, Jefferson Davis, who had been unanimously endorsed as the provisional president of the Confederacy, had spoken in Montgomery, Alabama. He was in no doubt that "a reunion with the States from which we have separated is neither practicable nor desirable". Lincoln disagreed. In his address on 4 March 1861, with Stephen Douglas, aware of the looming crisis, murmuring his approval, the new president appealed to the South. He had "no purpose … to

Below: Lincoln delivers his Gettysburg address. He is just visible, wearing a top hat, in the centre of the photograph.

HABEAS CORPUS

Lincoln controversially suspended the right of habeas corpus early in the Civil War. The Constitution permitted this when "in Cases of Rebellion or Invasion the public safety may require it", but the president faced legal challenges to his action, which he ignored, allowing his critics to argue that he had abused his presidential powers. Suspension gave the administration the right to arrest suspects without subsequently producing them before a court to determine if they had been legally detained. In the Confederacy, Jefferson Davis also suspended habeas corpus and declared martial law.

interfere with the institution of slavery in the States where it exists. I believe I have no lawful right to do so, and I have no inclination to do so." At the same time, Lincoln was adamant that the Confederacy had no constitutional status: "No State upon its own mere motion can lawfully get out of the

Below: Lincoln (centre) and his bodyguard Pinkerton (left) and General McClellan at Antietam, 1862.

Union ... the central idea of secession is the essence of anarchy." Furthermore, "In your hands, my dissatisfied fellow-countrymen, and not in mine, is the momentous issue of civil war."

CIVIL WAR

Little more than a month later, on 12 April, the war started. Following a Confederate bombardment, federal forces in Fort Sumter, South Carolina, surrendered. There were no fatalities.

Above: As the 'Savior of the Union' and the 'Great Emancipator', Lincoln rapidly became regarded as one of the greatest American presidents.

On 15 April Lincoln issued a proclamation calling on the states to raise a 75,000-strong militia. Two days later, Virginia announced it would secede. The decision was endorsed in a popular referendum held the following month. Arkansas, North Carolina and Tennessee followed. In a bold extension of presidential authority, Lincoln suspended habeas corpus, blockaded Southern ports, and increased the size of the regular army and navy. At the end of April, the Confederate Constitution was ratified, and Jefferson Davis called Lincoln's proclamation mobilizing the militia a "declaration of war".

On 4 July Lincoln sent a message to Congress, focusing on events in a Southern state bordering Washington DC: "The people of Virginia have thus allowed this giant insurrection to make its nest within her borders, and this Government has no choice but to deal with it where it finds it." Thomas Jefferson's home state was about to become the principal theatre in America's Civil War.

THE EMANCIPATION PROCLAMATION

On 1 January 1863, President Lincoln issued the Emancipation Proclamation, declaring that "all persons held as slaves" in the states that had seceded "are, and henceforward shall be free". It did not extend to those slaves in the border states that had remained loyal and those parts of the Confederacy that the Union had occupied. Nevertheless, the Proclamation changed the character of the Civil War, which became not only a struggle against secession but also one for the freedom of those whom the South had enslaved.

It began badly for the Union. There was little to celebrate in 1861, as Confederate forces consolidated their hold on Virginia. There was no telling how it would end, but in his Annual Message to Congress in December, Lincoln made it clear that, "In considering the policy to be adopted for suppressing the insurrection, I have been anxious and careful that the inevitable conflict for this purpose shall not degenerate into a violent and remorseless revolutionary struggle." From the Confederacy's perspective, that is what it became.

In 1862, North and South traded blows at the Battles of Shiloh, Bull Run (for a second time), Antietam and Fredericksburg. It was after Antietam, on 22 September, that Lincoln announced his intention to issue the Emancipation Proclamation on the forthcoming New Year's Day. On 1 January 1863, he was true to his word: the slaves would be free, provided he won the war.

In July 1863 the Battle of Gettysburg proved to be a turning point in the war: the Union victory forced the Confederacy on to the defensive for the remainder of the conflict. In his Gettysburg address at the ceremonies dedicating the battlefield as a military cemetery, Lincoln gave a powerful and compelling justification of the need to fight and to preserve the principles of America's republican democracy.

Still the war dragged on. In 1864, Lincoln was re-nominated for a second term. His Democrat opponent was one of his former generals, George McClellan, and with Union morale at a low ebb, it seemed that the president might lose the election. In September, Confederate forces abandoned Atlanta, and Lincoln's political fortunes revived. In November, he defeated McClellan decisively in the election. By the time of his second inauguration in March

Above: Lincoln conferring with his military commanders. As commander-in-chief, he took responsibility for Union strategy.

1865, he looked confidently to the future: "With malice towards none, with charity for all … let us strive to finish the work we are in, to bind up the nation's wounds." A month later the Civil War was over. The Confederate surrender at Appomattox Courthouse in Virginia came on 9 April. Abraham Lincoln had succeeded.

Five days later, the president was immortalized by an assassin's bullet. President Abraham Lincoln died on 15 April 1865.

STATES ENTERING THE UNION DURING LINCOLN'S PRESIDENCY:

WEST VIRGINIA	NEVADA

Entered the Union: 20 June 1863
Pre-state history: Part of Virginia; remained in Union after outbreak of Civil War (1861)
Total population in 1870 census: 442,014
Electoral College votes in 1864: 5

Entered the Union: 31 October 1864
Pre-state history: Part of western Utah Territory; organized as Nevada Territory (1861)
Total population in 1860 census: 42,491
Electoral College votes in 1864: 2

JEFFERSON DAVIS
CONFEDERATE PRESIDENT

Around the time that Abraham Lincoln was born in a log cabin in Kentucky, the Davis family left the state. Unlike the Lincoln family, who later moved north, they headed south, eventually settling in the state of Mississippi. With them was the youngest of their ten children: Jefferson Davis, born in June 1808 and named for the author of the Declaration of Independence.

Davis's great-grandfather had emigrated from Wales to Pennsylvania in the 18th century, and his grandfather had settled in Georgia. During the War of Independence, his father, Samuel Davis, joined the Patriot militia, taking part in the Siege of Savannah. Two of his elder brothers served with Andrew Jackson's forces in the War of 1812. Davis had more formal education than Lincoln, returning to Kentucky and completing his studies at Transylvania College before entering the United States Military Academy, at West Point, as a cadet in 1824.

In 1831 he was involved in the Black Hawk War, in which Abraham Lincoln had volunteered for the militia. Three

Born: 3 June 1808, Christian County, Kentucky
Parents: Samuel (1756–1824) and Jane (1759–1845)
Family background: Farming
Education: West Point (1824)
Religion: Episcopal
Occupation: Soldier, planter
Slave owner: Yes
Political career: US House of Representatives, 1845–6
US Senate, 1847–51
Secretary of War, 1853–7
US Senate, 1857–61
Political party: Democrat
Died: 6 December 1889, New Orleans, Louisiana

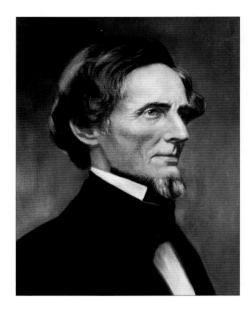

Above: The Confederacy existed for four years and during that time Jefferson Davis was its only president.

years later, he resigned his commission, not least because his future wife's father, Zachary Taylor, who had first-hand experience of the difficulties of family life in the military, opposed her involvement with a career soldier. He married Sarah Taylor in June. Three months later she died from malaria.

Davis spent the next decade growing cotton on his plantation near Vicksburg Mississippi, where he owned more than a hundred slaves. In 1845 he went to Washington as a member of the House of Representatives, and in the same year he married Varina Howell. They had six children.

Unlike Lincoln, Davis favoured the annexation of Texas. When war broke out with Mexico, he resigned his seat and rejoined the military. He fought alongside his former father-in-law, General Taylor, at the Battle of Buena Vista, where he was badly wounded.

In 1847, he entered the federal Senate. Although firmly identified with the politics of pro-slavery, he still favoured the South staying within the

United States, although he opposed elements of the 1850 Compromise. In 1851 he left Washington, contesting and narrowly losing the election for governor of Mississippi.

Returning to federal politics as Franklin Pierce's secretary of war, he was a leading supporter of the Kansas–Nebraska Act. When James Buchanan took office, Davis went back to the Senate and remained there until 21 January 1861. After Mississippi had voted for secession, he made his farewell speech. The South, he said, had history on its side: "When you deny us the right to withdraw from a Government which … threatens to be destructive of our rights, we but tread in the path of our fathers when we proclaim our independence and take the hazard."

A LOSING BATTLE

Given his military experience, Davis would have preferred to have been made commander-in-chief of the

Below: Davis had argued against secession while a senator, but was nevertheless inaugurated as president of the Confederacy.

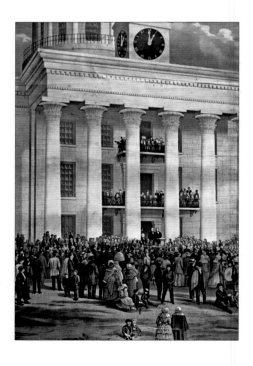

Above: In 1862, Davis appointed Robert E. Lee (seated at table) as his chief military advisor in planning the Confederacy's campaigns.

Confederacy's armies rather than its president. Instead he was first appointed to that office in February 1861, and then elected, without opposition, in November that year. He could not overcome the problems of infrastructure, economics and politics that would ultimately undermine the Confederacy. There was no integrated transport network: railroads had been constructed merely to allow cotton to be exported, rather than to facilitate movement between Southern states. The South's predominantly agricultural economy could not compete with the North's industrial production once that was organized to support the Union war effort.

During the Civil War the South's financial position lurched from precarious to parlous as it experienced rampant inflation.

Believing that Britain, which relied on the South for most of its cotton, would be a natural ally, Davis underestimated the opposition to slavery across the Atlantic, where British workers had little sympathy for the Confederate cause. Foreign governments refused to recognize his administration, which remained isolated throughout the Civil War. Within the Confederacy, he found it difficult to exercise centralized authority, as rival states jealously guarded their political autonomy.

Davis toured the South trying to boost morale, but he could not postpone its complete political, economic and military collapse. Having escaped Union forces advancing on Richmond, he was captured on 10 May 1865 and imprisoned at Fort Monroe in Virginia. Indicted for treason the following year, he was released on bail in 1867. In 1868, the case was dropped. He survived for 21 years, widely respected in the South as a symbol of its 'Lost Cause'. On 6 December 1889 Jefferson Davis died in New Orleans.

THE 'LOST CAUSE'

Soon after the surrender at Appomattox, the South began to rationalize its defeat and to recover its sense of honour through the concept of the 'Lost Cause'. This movement emphasized the leadership qualities of Davis, Robert E. Lee and 'Stonewall' Jackson, among others, together with the endeavours of Confederate troops as they had heroically resisted the Union's attack on their homeland. With the United States anxious to avoid recriminations over slavery, the defeated Confederacy emerged victorious in the battles over how the Civil War was to be remembered.

Above: Lee surrendered to Grant at the end of the Civil War. Though the battle was lost, Lee's stature was assured.

THE CIVIL WAR
1861–1865

Why did they fight? For the Union, Southern secession threatened to destroy the 'idea of America' expressed in the Declaration of Independence and enshrined in the Constitution of 1787: a republic based upon the democratic principles of equality and liberty. For the South, the prospect of invasion from the North, in order to force it back into the political and constitutional frame-work that it had finally rejected, mobilized its resistance and explained its persistence. Early in the conflict a Confederate prisoner of war was asked why he had taken up arms. His reply was simple: "I'm fighting because you're down here." For almost four years, the Blue and the Gray – the colours adopted by the Union and the Confederacy – battled with one another in what remains the fiercest and most compelling conflict in American history.

START OF THE WAR
After the Battle of Fort Sumter, in which the Union troops surrendered, no serious confrontations took place until July 1861. Then, at the Battle of First Manassas (Bull Run) in Northern Virginia, the Confederates, commanded by General Pierre Beauregard, won, forcing Union troops and civilian spectators who had come from Washington to witness the action into a disorderly retreat. In Southern mythology, this was where one of its most famous generals, 'Stonewall' Jackson, won his nickname. Appearing not to panic in the confusion

Above: In April 1863 the price of wheat tripled, leading starving women to riot over the price of bread.

of the battlefield, he set an example to the rest. Lincoln swiftly removed General Irving McDowell, who was held responsible for this setback as commander of the army of the Potomac. His replacement, George McClellan, proved reluctant to engage the enemy and risk further failure. The momentum of the conflict stalled.

By January 1862, Lincoln faced increasing public discontent over the lack of military action. There were concerns about the rising costs of keeping a 700,000-strong army in the field. McClellan was suffering from typhoid fever. In conversation with Montgomery Meigs, the quartermaster general of the Union army, the president gloomily observed: "The bottom is out of the tub."

In March, the architecture of naval warfare changed. 'Ironclads' (armour-plated ships) were used for the first time. The *Merrimack*, an old Union frigate salvaged by the Confederates and renamed the *Virginia*, was fitted out with armour plating and took on with ease the Union navy's wooden ships that

---

KEY BATTLES OF THE CIVIL WAR

Fort Sumter: 12–13 April 1861, near Charleston, South Carolina. Bombardment of Union fort that began Civil War.

First Manassas (Bull Run): 21 July 1861, Virginia. Confederate victory.

Wilson's Creek: 10 August 1861, Springfield, Missouri. First major battle west of the Mississippi, won by Confederates and the Missouri State Guard.

Fort Donelson: 12–16 February 1862, Stewart County, Tennessee. Union victory.

Pea Ridge: 7–8 March 1862, near Bentonville, Arkansas. Union victory, gaining control of Missouri.

Hampton Roads: 8–9 March 1862, naval battle, notable as the first encounter between ironclads.

Shiloh: 6–7 April 1862, south-west Tennessee. Union victory.

New Orleans: 25 April–1 May 1862. Bloodless capture of largest Confederate city.

Seven Days Battles: 25 June–1 July 1862, near Richmond, Virginia. Confederate victory.

Second Manassas (Bull Run): 28–30 August 1862. Confederate victory.

Antietam: 17 September 1862, near Sharpsburg, Maryland. First major battle on Northern soil.

Fredericksburg: 11–15 December 1862, Virginia. Confederate victory.

Chancellorsville: 30 April–6 May 1863, Spotsylvania Courthouse, Virginia. Confederate victory.

Gettysburg: 1–3 July 1863, Pennsylvania. Union victory and turning point of the war.

Vicksburg: 18 May–4 July 1863, Mississippi. Union victory.

Chattanooga: 23–25 November, 1863, Tennessee. Union victory.

Atlanta: 22 July 1864. Union victory. City razed on 11 November.

Five Forks: 1 April 1865, near Petersburg, Virginia. Union victory leading to Confederate retreat.

were enforcing Lincoln's blockade of Southern ports, until the Union's equivalent, the *Monitor*, purpose built and better designed, arrived. The blockade was preserved.

The following month, at Shiloh in Tennessee, Union forces commanded by Ulysses S. Grant survived a surprise Confederate attack. It established the pattern of war: battles were decided by a combination of the competence, or lack of it, of the generals on both sides and the heroic, sometimes futile, sacrifice of their troops: the number of casualties, killed and wounded, was both appalling and terrifying.

ROBERT E. LEE

In June 1862, the most talented of the Confederacy's generals, Robert E. Lee, took command of the army of Northern Virginia. He replaced Joseph Johnston, who had been wounded at the Battle of Seven Pines, and whose reluctant approach to the war had made him an apt opponent for the equally

THE CONFEDERATE FLAG

The Confederate states had more than one flag in the four years between 1861 and 1865. The first flag (pictured top right) known as the Stars and Bars was shown with between seven and 15 stars. The second flag, the Stainless Banner (held by the soldier) was also the battle flag. It was displayed on a white background (middle right), but at sea was thought to look like a flag of truce, so the red vertical bar was added (bottom right).

Above: The second Battle of Bull Run involved tens of thousands of men on each side and was a major engagement in the Civil War.

cautious McClellan, whose army of the Potomac remained aloof from the conflict. Two months later Lee inflicted a crushing defeat on General John Pope's army of Virginia at the Battle of Second Manassas (Bull Run). In September he took the fight to the North, but at the Battle of Antietam in Maryland, amid scenes of widespread slaughter on both sides, the Union claimed victory. Lincoln sacked McClellan for refusing to press home his advantage, only to see his replacement, General Ambrose Burnside, advance into Virginia and lose the Battle of Fredericksburg.

During 1862 the war in the West ebbed and flowed. Grant's campaign, deep in Confederate territory, was disrupted by the guerrilla tactics of Nathan Forrest, who became one of the most successful cavalry commanders during the war, and forced Grant to abandon an attempt to capture the strategically important town of Vicksburg on the Mississippi River. In May 1863, Grant regained the initiative, winning five battles in three weeks, but his exploits appeared as supporting acts to the unfolding drama in the East. The fighting in Northern Virginia, between Washington and the Confederate capital of Richmond, was coupled with the occasional Southern foray into Union

territory. It was here that the most important battle of the war took place, not on Confederate soil but in Pennsylvania, at Gettysburg.

DEATH OF A GENERAL

In Virginia in May 1863, Lee defeated Burnside's replacement, Joseph Hooker, at the Battle of Chancellorsville. The victory was marred by the death of Stonewall Jackson, who was a victim of friendly fire. Afterwards, Lee moved his army north. By invading Union territory he hoped to relieve the military pressure being exerted by Grant in the West, finally to destroy the army of the Potomac, and maybe to capture Washington itself, forcing European powers to recognize the Confederacy as an independent nation.

Meanwhile Hooker clashed with Henry Halleck, whom Lincoln had appointed general in chief of the Union armies in July 1862. Forced to choose between them, the president replaced Hooker with General George Meade. Within three days he faced Lee at Gettysburg.

GETTYSBURG

The battle began on 1 July. For two days, the Union army resisted Confederate attacks. When the battle recommenced on the afternoon of 3 July, in Lee's words it "raged with great violence until sunset". During this decisive phase, General James Longstreet, who later claimed he had been reluctant to do so, gave Lee's order to attack Union forces ranged on Cemetery Ridge. Pickett's charge was Lee's military gamble, and he lost. Union artillery and troops repulsed the assault, with the Confederates sustaining heavy casualties. It was the beginning of the end.

UNION ADVANCES

It rained at Gettysburg on Independence Day that year and no significant fighting took place there. In the West, however, Grant finally captured Vicksburg. On 5 July the survivors of the Confederate army in Pennsylvania started the retreat to Virginia. Southern morale received a temporary boost with victory at the Battle of Chickamauga in Tennessee in September, but before the year ended, Grant won the Battle of Chattanooga and the state was in Union hands.

In March 1864, Grant became only the second officer to be promoted to the rank of lieutenant general; the first had been George Washington, taking overall command of the armies of the United States.

The Civil War had entered its final phase. In Virginia, the Wilderness Campaign became a relentless struggle of attrition. The army of the Potomac sustained more than 50,000 casualties as it advanced slowly into Confederate territory, and some of Lee's key generals were killed, wounded or captured as his Confederate army suffered proportionately similar losses.

On 2 September, General William Tecumseh Sherman captured Atlanta, a critical Confederacy citadel. He wrote to Grant, outlining his next move: "If you can whip Lee and I can march to the Atlantic, I think Uncle Abe will give us twenty days leave of absence to see the young folks". Grant's grim struggle in Virginia was complemented by Sherman's purposeful destruction of Confederate resources further South during his famous 'march to the sea' in the closing months of 1864.

THE END OF THE WAR

The final acts of war were swift. On 3 April 1865, Union troops occupied Richmond. President Lincoln visited the former Confederate capital, spending time in Jefferson Davis's study less than two days after his rival had hastily vacated it. On 9 April he arrived back in Washington. On the same day, in Virginia, at Appomattox Courthouse, a mud-spattered Lee surrendered to Grant, who was resplendent in his military uniform.

It was just under four years since the war had begun with the shelling of Fort Sumter. General Lee wrote to Jefferson Davis: "I did not see how a surrender could be avoided. We had no subsistence for man or horse, and it could not be gathered in the country. The supplies could not reach us, and the men, deprived of food and sleep for many days, were worn out and exhausted." So, too, was the Confederacy.

Grant would later recall the end of the war as a low-key affair in which he had been careful to treat Lee with respect, refusing to demand that the defeated leader give up his sword as a symbol of the Confederacy's capitulation. The hope was that the two sides could embark on a path towards reconciliation after what had been, for both of them, a brutal and costly conflict. Binding up the nation's wounds would not be easy. On 11 April Lincoln gave what proved to be his last public address. He was aware that "the re-inauguration of the national authority – reconstruction – which has had a large share of thought from the first, is pressed much more closely upon our attention. It is fraught with great difficulty." Among his audience was John Wilkes Booth. Three days later he fired the fatal shot: Abraham Lincoln, who had done so much to ensure that the United States survived the Civil War, became its most famous casualty.

THE ASSASSINATION OF LINCOLN

On the evening of 14 April 1865, Good Friday, Abraham Lincoln, accompanied by his wife, went to Ford's Theatre in Washington to watch a performance of the comedy, *Our American Cousin.* Ulysses S. Grant had turned down an invitation to share the president's box. In the play's third act, the 26-year-old John Wilkes Booth shot Lincoln in the head at close range. He jumped down on to the stage, catching his spur on the American flag decorating the box and injuring himself in the process, shouted the motto of Virginia, "*Sic semper tyrannis*" ("Thus always to tyrants") and escaped. This was an assassin who never intended to remain anonymous, and an actor who would be forever remembered for that one performance.

Lincoln did not regain consciousness. He died at 7.22 a.m. the following morning. Edwin Stanton, the secretary of war, witnessed the president's final moments, and observed: "Now he belongs to the ages." The news caused consternation in the South, which expected both blame and reprisals when it became evident that the assassin had not acted on a whim nor alone.

THE SEARCH FOR THE MURDERERS

Booth was hunted down and killed while trying to resist arrest. Private John Millington was present when the assassin was cornered in a barn near Port Royal, Virginia: "He refused to come out … I heard a shot and a moment later saw the door was open. Booth had been shot through the neck."

Afterwards the conspiracy was pieced together. On 13 April, a stranger had appeared at Edwin Stanton's house, where General Grant was visiting. He had asked that both the secretary of war and his guest be pointed out to him. The following evening Booth had visited the hotel where the vice president, Andrew Johnson, was staying, leaving a card and the message: "Don't wish to disturb you. Are you at home? J. Wilkes Booth." While the well-mannered assassin went to find Lincoln, two accomplices, Lewis Powell and David Herold, arrived at the home of the secretary of state, William Seward. Powell forced his way into Seward's bedroom and stabbed him a number of times before escaping.

In the immediate aftermath of the assassination, Stanton sent investigators to the home of Mary Surratt, where Booth was known to stay while in Washington. When they returned to question her late on the night of 17 April, Powell arrived with a pick-axe. Surratt refused to corroborate his story that she had hired him to dig a gutter, and both were arrested. Powell was quickly identified as Seward's assailant.

By then there had been three other arrests: Edman Spangler, seen with Booth before the assassination, Samuel Arnold, also linked to Booth by incriminating correspondence, and Michael O'Laughlen, a childhood friend of Booth's, who had allegedly been given the task of assassinating Stanton, but had not carried it out.

On 20 April George Atzerodt, who was suspected of being a conspirator, was taken into custody. He had been seen at the vice president's hotel on the day of the assassination and evidence was found connecting him to Booth. Samuel Mudd, the doctor who treated Booth's broken leg, was arrested as a member of the conspiracy and David Herold, who had helped Booth to Mudd's house, was also captured.

They were tried by a military commission. On 30 June 1865 all were found guilty of at least one of the conspiracy charges brought against them. Surratt, Powell, Atzerodt and Herold received the death sentence. Arnold, Mudd and O'Laughlen were given life imprisonment with hard labour. Spangler was jailed for six years. The remaining suspect, Mary Surratt's son, John Jr, was apprehended in Egypt the following year.

Lincoln's funeral took place on 19 April 1865. After ceremonies in the East Room of the White House, his body lay in state at the Capitol before being taken back to Springfield, Illinois, where he was finally laid to rest.

Below: Lincoln's assassination ensured his reputation as one of America's finest presidents. For his successors, the political landscape had been permanently changed as a result of the catharsis of Civil War.

97

ANDREW JOHNSON
1865–1869

Andrew Johnson was born in a log cabin in North Carolina. He had less formal education than Lincoln, but he did have a trade. Johnson was the first president not to have pursued a career in either the law or the military. He was apprenticed as a tailor in 1822, and four years later, not yet 18 and still illiterate, arrived in Greeneville, Tennessee, where he opened for business. In 1827, he married Eliza McCardle, the 16-year-old daughter of the local cobbler. She helped him learn to read and write.

By 1834, he had become an alderman, then mayor of Greeneville. A southern Democrat and a slave-owner, his career in state and national politics took him first to the Tennessee State Legislature, then to the House of Representatives in Washington, then back to the office of state governor for

Above: Andrew Johnson was from that part of Tennessee which remained loyal to the Union despite the state's secession. His presidency was not highly regarded.

Republicans alike. Above all, Andrew Johnson was not Abraham Lincoln.

Extreme Republicans expected the defeated Confederacy to suffer. More moderate opinion favoured the Southern states' restoration to the Union under terms decided by the federal Congress. Lincoln himself had considered the simple option of using the executive power of pardon to bring the South back into the Union, believing that constitutionally the rebel states had never ceased to be part of the United States.

RECONSTRUCTION MEASURES

Johnson adopted Lincoln's agenda for reconstruction and swiftly moved it forward. Provisional governors were appointed in the former Confederacy, new constitutions abolishing slavery were written and, once they were ratified, states were allowed representation in Washington. This strategy fell apart as soon as Congress reconvened: the Republicans refused to admit Southern representatives or to recognize the reconstituted state governments.

The legislature was reasserting its power after deferring to the executive during the war years. In April 1866, Johnson's veto of a Civil Rights Act giving citizenship to all those born in the United States (it had also included Native Americans but had not given them voting rights) was overturned.

Born: 29 December 1808, Raleigh, North Carolina
Parents: Jacob (1778–1812) and Mary (1783–1856)
Family background: Labouring
Education: Not formally educated
Religion: Not proclaimed
Occupation: Tailor, public official
Slave owner: Yes – but not while president
Political career: Alderman, Greeneville, Tennessee, 1830–3
Mayor, Greeneville, Tennessee, 1834
Tennessee State Legislature, 1835–43
US House of Representatives, 1843–53
Governor of Tennessee, 1853–7
US Senate, 1857–62, 1875
Military Governor of Tennessee, 1862–5
Vice president, 1865
Presidential annual salary: $25,000
Political party: Democrat
Died: 31 July 1875, Carter's Station, Tennessee

Tennessee, and in 1857 to the federal Senate. East Tennessee, Johnson's home, was an area of the country where there was a strong abolitionist sentiment and a majority of the local population were opposed to the state's secession. It stayed loyal to the Union. In 1861, Johnson remained in Washington, the only southern senator not to resign his seat. The following year he was appointed military governor of Tennessee.

In 1864, seeking to broaden his electoral base among pro-Union Democrats, President Lincoln sacked his vice president, Hannibal Hamlin, in favour of Johnson, who served in that position for just 11 days. He inherited the office on 15 April 1865, and with it the problems of post-Civil War reconstruction, where his approach ran aground on the implacable rock of congressional opposition. He faced several political disadvantages. As a southerner who had remained loyal to the Union, he was mistrusted in the former Confederacy and by Northern

---

ELIZA JOHNSON

Eliza McCardle was born in Tennessee in 1810 and married Andrew Johnson in 1826. They had five children. Illness restricted her public appearances as first lady, so her daughters took on that role. She died in 1876, six months after her husband, and four months before their 50th wedding anniversary.

Two months later, Congress enshrined this principle in the Fourteenth Amendment to the Constitution and made Southern states' acceptance of it a pre-condition for readmission. In that year's mid-term elections, Republicans won two-thirds majorities in the House and the Senate.

The following year Johnson's veto of the Reconstruction Act, introducing military government and martial law

Below: In 1864 Johnson, a southern Democrat, broadened the Republican ticket's appeal at a critical stage of the war.

in the South, was also overturned. Congress assumed the right to decide when former Confederate states might rejoin the Union. Seven had met the strict criteria for readmission by June 1868. Only Virginia, Mississippi, Texas and Georgia were still excluded.

IMPEACHMENT
In the acrimonious political atmosphere, Johnson provoked his own impeachment trial by reasserting the president's power to remove federal officials without congressional approval. He sacked Edwin Stanton as secretary of war.

STATES ENTERING THE UNION UNDER JOHNSON: NEBRASKA

Entered the Union: 8 February 1867
Pre-state history: Organized as Nebraska Territory (1854)
Total population in 1870 census: 122,993
Electoral College votes in 1868: 3

On 24 February 1868, the House of Representatives approved the articles of impeachment by a vote of 126 to 47. In the Senate trial, with the chief justice of the Supreme Court, Salmon Chase, presiding, Johnson's opponents three times fell short by a single vote of the two-thirds majority necessary for conviction. Although it failed, impeachment achieved Congress's desired result: the president had no effective political influence for the remainder of his time in office. Following his impeachment, he failed to gain the Democrats' nomination in the 1868 presidential election.

Johnson died in July 1875, a few months after he had returned to the Senate, where his impeachment trial had so nearly brought an ignominious end to his presidency.

Below: Johnson survived impeachment when the Senate vote fell one short of the majority needed for conviction.

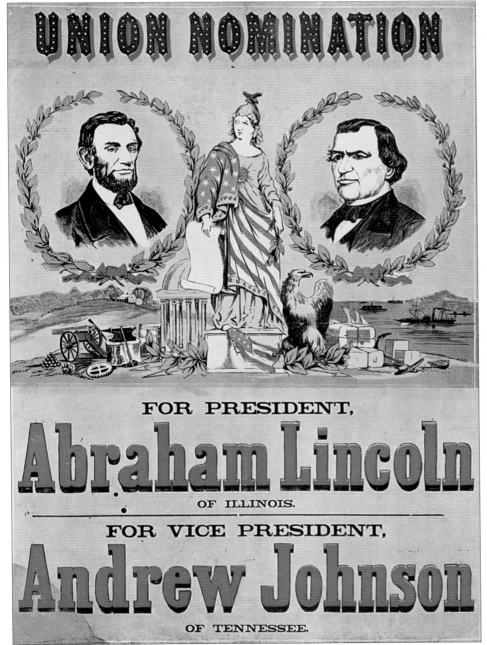

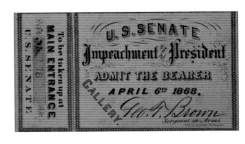

RECONSTRUCTION

Could the South change? Would the society that had embraced slavery be able to transcend its history of discrimination? Confederate ghosts continued to haunt many Southern attics: it would be another century before the Civil Rights movement forced fundamental alterations to the attitudes that were preserved there.

THE FREEDMEN'S BUREAU

With President Johnson encouraging the initial pace of reconstruction during 1865, restoring the Confederate states to the Union was more important than establishing civil rights for former slaves. Congress established the Bureau of Refugees, Freedmen and Abandoned Lands, known as the Freedmen's Bureau, to assist them. Its most notable achievement was the setting up of schools and colleges for the children of freedmen, but it was underfunded and faced mounting opposition.

Below: The Ku Klux Klan used tactics of violence and intimidation in its campaign for white supremacy.

Several Southern states implemented strict 'Black Codes' to ensure the continued social, political and economic exclusion of the black population. Most of these codes left only agricultural labour and domestic work open to blacks. They were not allowed to raise their own crops, to lease land or to live in towns and cities without the consent of a white employer.

The Ku Klux Klan was formed, with former Confederate officers among its leaders – Nathan Forrest was its first Grand Wizard – and Southern white supremacists persisted in their acts of racial terrorism until, in 1871, congressional action temporarily curbed their activities. The Ku Klux Klan reformed in 1915: its intimidating white-hooded regalia, its practice of burning crosses and its predilection for lynchings became powerful symbols of the South's continuing violent reaction to any prospect of racial integration.

CARPETBAGGERS AND SCALAWAGS

The collapse of the Confederate National Government and many state governments had left a legislative vacuum. The 1867 Reconstruction Act passed by the Radical Republicans reorganized ten former Confederate states into five military districts, each under the direct control of a US army general. The army either appointed its own officers to government posts or supervised elections and safeguarded the elected officials.

Meanwhile, a host of Northerners travelled south to take part in the reconstruction. They were characterized as 'carpetbaggers' because they travelled light – implying that they were not intending to stay long – carrying their possessions in inexpensive luggage. Some were abolitionists full of reforming zeal, who went to join the struggle

Above: 'Carpetbaggers' travelled south with all their worldly possessions, often hoping to exploit the economic opportunities of reconstruction.

for racial equality, others were teachers and missionaries who worked with the freed slaves and their children, often as the employees of the Freedmen's Bureau. But there were many others, including former Union soldiers, who were attracted by the economic opportunities opening up in the South, where the infrastructure had been left in a state of chaos, and it was from them that the term 'carpetbagger' derived its derogatory sense of an outsider who meddles in the politics of a region for personal gain.

The incomers made fortunes by buying up cotton plantations and using freedmen as hired labour, and largely took control of the Southern railroads. They formed the basis of the Republican party in the South, and together with indigenous white Republicans (who were pejoratively known by their opponents as 'scalawags', a term for disreputable and unprincipled scoundrels) and blacks elected to political office, they monopolized positions of political power.

A PLACE APART

The Fourteenth Amendment to the Constitution had extended citizenship to blacks in 1866; the Fifteenth Amendment gave them the right to vote, though most of the Southern states found ways to restrict these rights. But by 1870, the Radical Republican effort to reconstruct the South was faltering. President Ulysses S. Grant and many of his contemporaries, as well as the generations succeeding them, accepted the price of a lasting peace: recognition that the South's sense of honour could ultimately only be recovered if the Civil War was seen as the Confederacy's valiant but losing fight for self-determination – the myth of the 'Lost Cause' – rather than as a struggle to end slavery.

Economic recession resulting from the panic of 1873 hit the Southern economy hard, as the price of cotton halved and small planters and merchants were bankrupted. Carpetbaggers returned to the North, and the Republican party in the South, which had given blacks a political voice,

PLESSY V. FERGUSON

The case of Plessy v. Ferguson (1896) was brought to test the constitutionality of a statute of Louisiana, which required railroads to provide separate accommodation for white and coloured passengers. Plessy had been arrested for refusing to move to the coloured section of the car.

The Supreme Court decided that if facilities were "separate but equal", then no constitutionally protected civil rights were infringed. In practice, this allowed the system of segregated institutions established in the South after the Civil War to remain in place. It was not until almost 60 years later that the Civil Rights movement finally managed to overturn the legal protection the Court had given to racial discrimination, forcing Southern states into desegregation.

Above: Supporters of the former Confederacy suffered under military occupation and resented the influx of carpetbaggers.

dwindled. As *The Nation*, which had begun publishing weekly in 1865 and which sympathized with the cause of civil rights, correctly prophesied after the election of President Rutherford B. Hayes: "The negro will disappear from the field of national politics. Henceforth, the nation, as a nation, will have nothing more to do with him." Shortly after Hayes entered the White House in 1877, the remaining federal troops in Southern states were recalled. Without their protection, black political participation came to an end, and Republicans were replaced by newly elected white Southern Democrats. Reconstruction, along with Republican political influence in the former Confederacy, was over.

As the 'Lost Cause' myth gained historical traction, the region, which was now dominated by conservative Democrats who would not vote for the party of Lincoln, continued to define itself in cultural and political terms as a place apart from the nation as a whole. Although slavery had been abolished, racism remained as a fundamental fault line in American politics, permeating attitudes on both sides of the Mason–Dixon line.

In 1896, the Supreme Court legitimized racial segregation throughout the American South in the case of Plessy v. Ferguson. It was a decision that the then president, Grover Cleveland, from New York, did not oppose. Black civil rights were ignored. The Confederate states had lost the war, but in many ways they had won the peace.

CHAPTER FIVE

ULYSSES S. GRANT TO WILLIAM MCKINLEY

1869–1901

SEVEN PRESIDENTS ENTERED THE WHITE HOUSE BETWEEN 1869 AND 1901. SIX WERE REPUBLICANS, FIVE WERE BORN IN OHIO, AND FOUR HAD SERVED IN CONGRESS. THREE WERE RE-ELECTED, TWO WERE ASSASSINATED. NONE OF THEM WAS FROM THE FORMER CONFEDERACY. FROM THE END OF THE CIVIL WAR TO THE TURN OF THE NEW CENTURY, THE UNITED STATES EXPERIENCED RAPID INDUSTRIALIZATION AND URBANIZATION, FUELLED BY ANOTHER WAVE OF PREDOMINANTLY EUROPEAN IMMIGRATION. IT WAS THE 'GILDED AGE', IN WHICH THE WEALTHY SAW CAPITALISM AS CONFIRMING CHARLES DARWIN'S THEORY OF EVOLUTION: "THE SURVIVAL OF THE FITTEST". VIOLENT CONFRONTATIONS BETWEEN WORKERS AND EMPLOYERS BECAME COMMONPLACE. WITHIN THE FEDERAL GOVERNMENT, CONGRESS ASSUMED A DOMINANT ROLE, BUT AS THE 19TH CENTURY DREW TO A CLOSE, PRESIDENTS BEGAN TO TAKE THE LEAD IN THE POLITICAL TRANSITIONS THAT ACCOMPANIED THE USA'S EMERGENCE AS A WORLD POWER.

Left: The meeting of the railways in Utah ensured westward expansion and heralded a new industrial era.

ULYSSES S. GRANT

1869–1877

After a turbulent military career, during which his critics alleged that his longest battle had been with the bottle, in 1868 General Ulysses S. Grant spent the accumulated political capital from his military defeat of the Confederacy in becoming the first president elected after the Civil War. He became the highest-ranking general in the United States army and the first president since Andrew Jackson to serve two full terms in the White House. Grant's political skills never matched his abilities as a soldier and he proved as incapable of mastering the intricacies of US politics as he had been successful in fighting the South's secession.

Born in Ohio in 1822, he won a scholarship to West Point Military Academy and embarked on an army career. With his natural affinity for horses and peerless skill in riding, Grant seemed destined for the cavalry, but disciplinary problems, coupled with low academic achievement (he graduated in 1843 in the bottom half of his class),

Above: A brilliant general but an unskilled politician, Grant's reputation was tainted by the widespread corruption in his administration.

meant he was assigned to the infantry instead. He served under Zachary Taylor in the Mexican War, and another of his superior officers was Robert E. Lee. By 1854, he had been promoted to captain, but his inability to accept army discipline, coupled with rumours of excessive drinking, led to a request for his resignation. He tried farming, but lost his land after a succession of crop failures. Then the Civil War came.

Back in the army, Grant impressed Lincoln with his coolness under fire, and his willingness to fight brought him regular promotions to positions of increasing military responsibility. In 1865 he accepted Robert E. Lee's surrender when the Confederacy collapsed. His status as a national hero made him an obvious choice as the Republican nominee for the presidential election of 1868. Grant won a

Right: The 1868 presidential election campaign was the first that took place during the reconstruction of the south.

convincing victory, defeating the Democrat candidate, Horatio Seymour, the governor of New York.

SCANDAL IN GOVERNMENT

Apart from Hamilton Fish, a former governor of New York who became his secretary of state, most of Grant's cabinet appointments did not serve him well. As president he proved vulnerable to manipulation by those less honest than himself. Two unscrupulous businessmen, Jay Gould and Jim Fisk, gained access to the president through his brother-in-law, Abel Corbin, and convinced him that he should restrict the sale of gold, while they cornered the market. When Grant finally worked out the scheme, he instructed the Treasury to sell government gold reserves, but there was financial panic on 24 September 1869 – 'Black Friday' – as the price of gold plummeted.

Born: 27 April 1822, Clermont County, Ohio
Parents: Jesse (1794–1873) and Hannah (1798–1883)
Family background: Leather tanning
Education: West Point Military Academy (1843)
Religion: Methodist
Occupation: Soldier
Slave owner: One slave inherited from father-in-law (later freed)
Political career: None prior to presidency
Presidential annual salary: $25,000, increased to $50,000 (1873)
Political party: Republican
Died: 23 July 1885, Mount McGregor, New York

JULIA GRANT

Born Julia Dent in 1826 on a Missouri plantation, she married Grant in 1848; her cousin, the future Confederate general James Longstreet, was one of the groom's attendants. The Grants had four children. Julia Grant revelled in being first lady, leaving the White House reluctantly. Her memoirs were finally published 73 years after her death in 1902.

Right: Julia Dent Grant, while first lady.

designs on the White House, and tried unsuccessfully to regain the Republican nomination in 1880. By 1884, speculative investments had failed. Facing mounting debt, and terminally ill with cancer of the throat, Grant took the advice of a friend, Mark Twain, and wrote the story of his remarkable life. He died just after he had completed his task, and the profits from the posthumous publication of his memoirs restored his family's fortune.

Other scandals emerged. In 1872, it became evident that the cost of building part of the Union Pacific Railroad had been massively inflated by the construction company, Credit Mobilier of America. The action created windfall profits for its owners, who also happened to be major stockholders in Union Pacific and some of whom either were or had been senior members of Grant's administration. As Grant's campaign for re-election entered its last weeks, newspapers reported that many leading politicians, including Schuyler Colfax, his vice president, who had failed to gain re-nomination, Colfax's replacement, Henry Wilson, and the future president James Garfield, were implicated in the affair. Grant survived: profiting from a divided Democrat opposition, he was re-elected in an electoral college landslide, but his presidency collapsed under the weight of charges of cronyism and corruption.

A WORSENING CRISIS

Renewed financial panic in 1873 led to economic recession. Two years later members of the administration, including Grant's private secretary, were exposed as members of the 'Whiskey Ring', diverting tax revenue from liquor into their own pockets. In 1876, William

Right: The election campaign of 1872 was designed to appeal to the working classes.

Belknap, secretary of war resigned rather than face impeachment charges relating to bribes received from American Indian agents. Later that year, Grant, who had been dissuaded from seeking a third term, admitted in his final message to Congress that: "It was my fortune, or misfortune, to be called to the office of Chief Executive without any previous political training … Failures have been errors of judgment, not of intent."

RETIREMENT

After his presidency Grant embarked on a successful world tour that served to rehabilitate his reputation. He still had

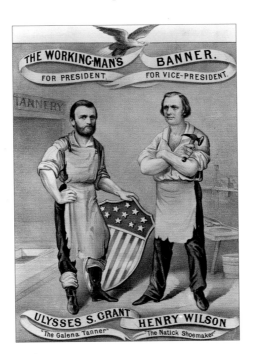

STATES ENTERING THE UNION DURING GRANT'S PRESIDENCY: COLORADO

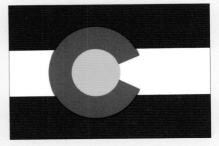

Entered the Union: 1 August 1876
Pre-state history: Part of Louisiana Purchase (1803) and land acquired from Mexico (1848); organized as Colorado Territory (1861)
Total population in 1880 census: 194,327
Electoral College votes in 1876: 3

'ROBBER BARONS'

The scandals that occurred during President Grant's administration were in part the product of the freewheeling world of post-Civil War US capitalism. Fortunes were made from industrialization, transportation, speculation and exploitation. Those able to take advantage of the opportunities on offer became either famous or notorious: sometimes both. In common with Andrew Carnegie, they started poor, or, like John Pierpoint Morgan, they inherited fortunes that they promptly increased. Their business empires, like those of John D. Rockefeller or Cornelius Vanderbilt, brought them wealth and power.

PHILANTHROPISTS

To their admirers, these architects of the USA's industrial economy were role models, demonstrating the potential of the 'American Dream': the myth that it was possible for everyone to rise in American society through talent and opportunity alone. Although some became famous for their philanthropy, to their critics they remained 'Robber Barons' – the economic opportunists who prospered in the free-for-all capitalism of the 'Gilded Age'.

ANDREW CARNEGIE

Born in 1835, Andrew Carnegie and his family emigrated from Scotland to Pennsylvania when he was 13. After initially working in a textile mill, in 1847 he became a telegraph messenger. He later joined the Pennsylvania Railroad as a telegraph operator, and by the time the Civil War broke out he had become superintendent of its Western Division. After spending the war in charge of Union telegraph communications, he saw the opportunities opening up in the steel industry to supply the track as the railroads expanded westwards. In 1875 he

Above: Carnegie realized that steel would replace iron as the metal of the future and built his fortune through investing in its production.

opened his first steel plant in Braddock, Pennsylvania, and his business interests expanded as his profits multiplied. By 1889 he was able to pay himself an annual salary of $25 million.

In 1900, at the age of 65, having built up the Carnegie Steel Company, Carnegie sold the business to J. P. Morgan for more than $400 million. Believing that "the accumulation of wealth should be followed by its distribution in the form of public endowments", he then proceeded to donate his fortune to numerous charitable causes, notably the foundation of libraries and other educational institutions. He died in 1919, one of the wealthiest and most generous philanthropists in American history.

Right: Rockefeller revolutionized the oil industry and amassed his personal fortune as the demand for oil increased.

J. P. MORGAN

During the Civil War, John Pierpoint Morgan was involved in a scheme to buy 5,000 obsolete rifles which, when refurbished, were resold to the Union army for a considerable profit. Born in 1837, the son of a financier, he inherited a fortune and increased it tenfold, using the family bank as the foundation of his

business empire. In 1891 he formed General Electric, the USA's principal manufacturer of electrical equipment.

In 1895 Morgan's financial influence was such that in order to save the USA's gold reserves, President Grover Cleveland was forced to allow him temporary but exclusive and hugely profitable control of the nation's gold trade. Having acquired Carnegie's steel company, Morgan created the United States Steel Corporation – the first billion-dollar industrial conglomerate.

At one time, Morgan held 72 directorships in 47 corporations. He was a passionate collector of books, works of art and gemstones. He died in 1913, having once confessed that "America is good enough for me." The comment provoked the Democrats' presidential candidate, William Jennings Bryan, to observe: "Whenever he doesn't like it, he can give it back to us."

JOHN D. ROCKEFELLER

The radical journalist Henry Demarest Lloyd once wrote that Standard Oil, John D. Rockefeller's corporation, had done everything to the Pennsylvania State Legislature except "refine it". Born in 1839, by the time he was 20 Rockefeller had set up in business for himself. After the Civil War he saw the potential of oil as the lubricant of the new industrial economy. In 1870 he established the Standard Oil Company of Ohio, and was its major shareholder. Within two decades, he had created a virtual monopoly.

Rockefeller's problem was not making money, but finding ways of spending it. He retired in 1897 and devoted himself to philanthropy: he was a major benefactor of the University of Chicago. By the time he died in 1937 he had succeeded in giving away most of his fortune.

CORNELIUS VANDERBILT

A member of an earlier generation than Carnegie, Morgan or Rockefeller, Cornelius Vanderbilt was born in 1794 and made his first fortune from steamboats on the Hudson River. Thenceforward known as 'the commodore', he turned his attention to railroads and by 1873 had established the rail link between New York and Chicago, creating one of America's most important transportation networks. During the economic depression of the same year, he built New York's Grand Central Station, providing employment for thousands of his fellow citizens. He died in 1877, leaving a fortune estimated at $100 million, at that time the largest in the United States.

Below: Vanderbilt built his fortune on the back of the industrial expansion that produced a need for steamships and railways.

THE DEVELOPMENT OF THE RAILROADS

In 1865 George Pullman built a sleeper car that set a new standard in comfort for long-distance rail travel. When one was attached to the funeral train carrying President Abraham Lincoln's body back to Illinois, it acted as an advertisement: the products of the Pullman Palace Car Company, based in Illinois, would become synonymous with transcontinental journeys by rail.

Railroads were the arteries of the USA's industrial age. Entrepreneurs, contractors and land speculators profited from building them. The Reno gang, from Indiana, had the dubious distinction of being the first to realize that railroads offered another source of income: in 1866 they boarded and robbed a train belonging to the Ohio and Mississippi Railroad.

THE TRANSCONTINENTAL RAILROAD

In 1850, Millard Fillmore approved the first Railroad Land Grant Act, allowing federal land to subsidize the construction of railroads in order to promote economic development and the settlement of the nation's interior. Abraham Lincoln, who had been a railroad lawyer in Illinois, granted more land to them than any other president. In 1862 he approved the first Pacific Railway Act, a critical step in creating the rail network that would link the east and west coasts of the United States. In deciding that the route west would start out from Omaha and be built by the newly formed Union Pacific, Lincoln enabled one of his former clients, Thomas Durant, the pivotal figure in

the Credit Mobilier scandal during Grant's presidency, to profit hugely from the government subsidies associated with the railroad's construction.

Initially, Durant was more concerned with financial wheeling and dealing than building the track, but eventually, using principally Irish immigrant workers, the Union Pacific Railroad began to make progress. The Central Pacific track was started in 1863 and was built east from Sacramento, mostly by Chinese immigrants. In 1869, the two tracks met at Promontory Summit in Utah. Further work was necessary before New York and San Francisco

Below: The Union Pacific and Central Pacific railroads met at Promontory Summit in Utah in 1869.

Above: The building of the railroads heralded the USA's industrial expansion.

were connected, but by June 1876 it was possible to travel between the two cities by train in less than four days.

SPECULATORS AND RAILROAD WORKERS

By the end of the 19th century, the US railroad system employed one in 20 of the nation's workforce. It had benefited from the gift of nearly 650,000 sq km (250,000 sq miles) of government land, and billions of dollars had been invested. Fortunes were made, mostly through the buying and selling of stock or by mergers and acquisitions.

The profits were in the construction rather than the operation of the rail network. From time to time, speculation and over-building helped to cause the economic recessions that recurred throughout the post-Civil War period. Many railroads went bankrupt, and they became political targets for those who saw them as rife with corruption. During his first term in the White House, Grover Cleveland made the railroads return more than 32 million ha (80 million acres) of government land

granted in the West, and also involved the federal government in trying to regulate the industry.

In 1893, as Cleveland began his second term and as another economic depression was deepening, 50 railway workers, meeting in Chicago, formed the American Railway Union. One of its leaders was Eugene Debs, born in

Below: As transport links increased the government used the railways as an incentive to move settlers west.

Above: Luxury Pullman cars carried affluent Americans across the US.

Indiana in 1855. He had been working on the railroads since the age of 14. In April 1894, soon after its formation, the union flexed its industrial muscle with a successful strike against the Great Northern Railway. A month later, the American Railway Union supported industrial action by Pullman workers protesting against a wage cut. In July, President Cleveland sent in federal troops to break the strike. The union's leaders, including Debs, were arrested. The following year they served seven months in jail for contempt of court.

The potential of the railroads seized the public's imagination. Nothing so dramatically symbolized the industrial and economic expansion of the United States as the building of an integrated rail network that linked its major cities. Travelling from coast to coast no longer required the heroic sacrifices of the pioneers who had struggled west in their covered wagons. Instead, it would be steel rails, steam locomotives and Pullman cars that opened up new opportunities for those restless to explore the North American continent.

THE GROWTH OF CITIES
AND POLITICAL MACHINES

When Thomas Jefferson became president in 1800, America was predominantly an agricultural nation. By 1896, when William McKinley occupied the White House, almost half the population of the United States lived in its cities, creating not only an energetic, dynamic and mobile society but also, in many urban centres, a new form of politics appropriate to the industrial age.

NEW YORK

From 1886 onwards, the first sight of America for the millions who came to the United States through the gateway of New York's Ellis Island immigration depot was the Statue of Liberty. Those who stayed in the city would soon find that it was the Democrat party organization, Tammany Hall, that dominated New York's political life.

The leaders of Tammany Hall saw what they did as 'honest graft': finding homes and jobs for newly arrived immigrants in return for their electoral support. That in turn brought them political capital and sources of patronage, and they became rich. To their critics, their organization and

Below: A newspaper cartoon depicting corrupt 'Boss' Tweed welcoming illness and disease into America.

exploitation of those fresh from the boats was a corrupting influence in US democracy.

One of Tammany's most infamous leaders was William 'Boss' Tweed, who effectively controlled New York City's finances before being convicted of fraud and sentenced to 12 years in prison. With Tweed jailed, the city's Irish Catholic community, which had fought long and hard against prejudice and exclusion, finally took over the machine. Irish 'bosses' controlled Tammany Hall from 1872 onwards, giving them a voice not only in the city, but also in state and national politics.

CHICAGO

The city of Chicago began as a frontier fort in the midst of some farmhouses. It became a town in 1833. By the 1870s Chicago's population was 300,000, and by the end of the century it would be well on the way to two million. After 1871, rising from the ashes of a destructive fire, Chicago rivalled New York in developing the iconic symbol of the US city: the skyscraper.

Above: The United States opened its doors to European immigrants, who entered through the processing depot on Ellis Island, New York.

During the 19th century, Chicago did not develop any highly organized political 'machines' like New York's Tammany Hall. It would not be until later in the 20th century that the Democrats managed to dominate the

TAMMANY HALL

Founded as a charity in 1789, within a decade the Tammany Society had become part of Aaron Burr's opposition to the Federalist party in New York. By the 1820s, it had established the practice of using the promise of delivering its members' votes as a way of gaining influence and political benefits. In 1830, the society moved its headquarters to Tammany Hall, the name that became synonymous with the Democrats' political machine in New York City.

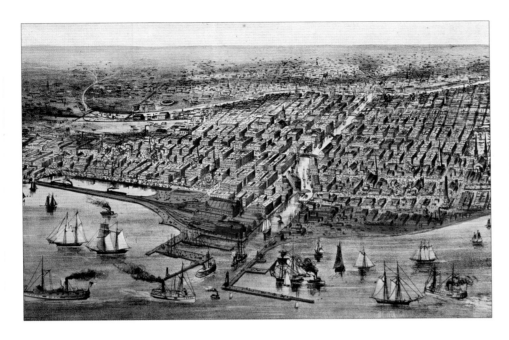

Above: New York in 1850 was a prosperous city for many.

Above: Chicago grew rapidly throughout the 19th century. Home to the world's first skyscraper, it revolutionized city planning.

mayor's office. Sometimes the city's politics seemed as combustible as its buildings had once been: in 1886, the Haymarket Riot led to the arrest and execution of anarchists accused of throwing a bomb that killed and injured police and protestors.

SAN FRANCISCO

Early in 1848, only a few hundred people lived in San Francisco; by the end of 1849 there were more than 30,000. It was built on the back of the Gold Rush. Over the next two years, six major fires destroyed it almost as quickly as it could be rebuilt. 'The wickedest city in the world' was a freewheeling place: in its red-light district, the Barbary Coast, brothels jostled with bars and dance halls competed with gambling houses, and in Chinatown there were thriving opium dens.

By the end of the 19th century, San Francisco had developed into a sophisticated city and had become the major urban financial and cultural centre of the Pacific coast. Its politics remained as corrupt as some of its morals. Nowhere was this better illustrated than in the career of Christopher Buckley, the city's 'Blind Boss' (he had lost his eyesight at the age of 30). He never held an elected office, but as the acknowledged leader of the San Francisco Democrats he ran the city's government for the last two decades of the century from his bar, the Alhambra, which was popularly known as 'Buckley's City Hall'.

POLITICS AND THE CITY

New York in the East, Chicago in the Midwest and San Francisco on the Pacific coast were three of the many US cities that grew as immigration, industrialization and the lure of the West transformed the landscape and shaped new forms of democratic politics. Cities meant votes. Political machines like Tammany Hall could deliver vital support for favoured local and national candidates. They were also where a new generation of US politicians learned their trade. Rising through the ranks of the Boston Democrat machine, in 1888 a second-generation Irish-American would give a nomination speech for Grover Cleveland at the Democrats' national convention. Seventy-two years later, Patrick Kennedy's grandson, benefiting from critical votes delivered by his party's Chicago political machine, became America's first Catholic president.

Left and below: Between 1850 (left) and 1875 (below) San Francisco's population burgeoned with the discovery of gold.

THE PRESIDENTIAL ELECTION
1876

The disputed presidential election of 1876 was one of the last convulsive aftershocks of the political earthquake of the Civil War. Unlike the two previous occasions when the electoral college had 'misfired', it was neither a tied vote nor the lack of a clear winner that confused the outcome. Having dissuaded Ulysses S. Grant from running for a third term, the Republicans won the disputed election only after an electoral commission that arbitrated the result voted on party lines and gave the White House to Rutherford B. Hayes.

The House of Representatives was not called upon to make the final decision. Instead Congress decided that a commission with five members from the House of Representatives, five members from the Senate and five Supreme Court justices would decide who should occupy the White House. Their choice of Hayes, the Republican candidate, was an accurate reflection of their partisan loyalties, but it was a distortion of democracy: his Democrat opponent, Samuel Tilden, had beaten him at the polls.

THE ELECTION AND ITS OUTCOME

Republican President Grant's administration, scandal-ridden and accident-prone, had grappled with the problems of reconstruction and a deteriorating economic climate and had lost the confidence of the nation. It had been 16 years since a Democrat had occupied the White House but in 1876, the party, which was increasingly entrenched in the South, made an electoral comeback in the rest of the country. The Democrats had the political sense to nominate Samuel Tilden for president. Not only was he from New York, which had the largest number of votes in the electoral college, he also had a reputation as a crusader against corruption, having successfully prosecuted 'Boss' Tweed of Tammany Hall. Thomas Hendricks from Indiana was selected as his running mate.

Rutherford Hayes was the former governor of Ohio, a Republican party stronghold. At the party's national convention, held in Cincinnati, he emerged as the compromise candidate, while William Wheeler from New York – inevitably – became the party's vice-presidential nominee.

The election campaign was close fought as well as controversial. Invective and insult dominated the debate. The Democrats seized on the issue of Republican corruption and the Republicans replied with an unsubtle reminder of recent history, goading their opponents with the slogan, "Not every Democrat was a Rebel, but every Rebel was a Democrat."

Tilden won the popular vote. He swept the South. With the support of New York and Indiana among other Northern and Midwestern states, he had 184 certain electoral college votes, one short of a majority. If he could gain the votes of South Carolina, Louisiana and Florida, which, like the rest of the former Confederacy, were regarded as Democrat states, he would be the clear winner. But there was one problem: those three states remained under military rule while reconstruction continued there. They also remained under Republican control.

Another controversy involved Oregon, where the Republican Hayes had won the popular vote. In the electoral college, one of the electors committed to vote for him held a federal office and so was disqualified from the proceedings on those grounds. The state's governor, who was a Democrat, appointed a substitute elector from his own party.

On 6 December, the electoral college convened in each state capital. In the three Southern states where both parties claimed that they had won the election, and in Oregon, Republican and

Left: Tilden being congratulated on becoming president: it was initially thought that he had won the election until events proved otherwise.

Democrat electors met and cast their votes separately, submitting two different ballot papers to Congress and leaving it to politicians in Washington to decide which one should be accepted as valid. Congress compromised, setting up the electoral commission that would arbitrate the result. Its members were carefully selected: there would be seven Democrats and seven Republicans who could be expected to vote on party lines. The 15th member, Supreme Court Justice David Davis, was appointed as an independent who would have the casting vote. Then he resigned amid charges of bribery and corruption. His replacement, Joseph Bradley, who was seen as the next most impartial justice after Davis, was nevertheless inclined towards the Republicans. His deciding vote meant that the commission awarded the disputed electoral college votes to Hayes. In such extraordinary circumstances, the Republicans retained control of the White House.

THE AFTERMATH

The result of the election was so transparently fraudulent that it immediately robbed Hayes of any semblance of political legitimacy as president. The Democrats initially threatened to obstruct the formal counting of the votes in the Senate, potentially leaving the outcome of the contest still undecided when Grant's term came to an end on 4 March 1877. It was not simply an act of political pique. There were rumours of a deal, although no official negotiations took place. Still, the circumstances of the election gave Southern Democrats some leverage. Soon after Hayes entered the White House, the remaining federal troops were recalled from the former Confederacy. Reconstruction was at an end. The Republicans effectively abandoned the South to the Democrats. Tilden retired from public life. As he observed, he had: "been elected to the highest position in the gift of the people, without any of the cares and responsibilities of the office."

Above: Congress determined that the presidential election should be decided by a specially appointed electoral commission.

Below: Democrats and Republicans contested electoral college votes mainly in Southern states still under military rule.

Key
C = Connecticut
D = Delaware
M = Massachusetts
Md = Maryland
N J = New Jersey
PA = Pennsylvania
R I = Rhode Island

Hayes

Tilden

RUTHERFORD HAYES
1877–1881

Rutherford Hayes was born in Ohio in October 1822 and was named in memory of his father, who died three months before his second son was born. His mother's brother helped to support the family thereafter. After obtaining his law degree from Harvard in 1845, Hayes returned to Ohio and became a successful criminal lawyer. In 1852, he married Lucy Webb, a graduate from a women's Methodist college in Cincinnati. They had eight children, five of whom survived to adulthood.

In 1853, influenced by his wife's anti-slavery convictions, Hayes began defending runaways escaping to the free state of Ohio across the Ohio River from Kentucky. He worked with Salmon Chase, later Lincoln's secretary of the treasury and chief justice of the Supreme Court. He served with distinction during the Civil War.

After the Whigs disintegrated, Hayes helped to organize the Republican party in Ohio, and won election to the

Born: 4 October 1822, Delaware, Ohio
Parents: Rutherford (1787–1822) and Sophia (1792–1866)
Family background: Farming, whiskey distilling
Education: Kenyon College (1842), Harvard Law School (1845)
Religion: Not proclaimed
Occupation: Lawyer
Military career: Major-General, Civil War
Political career: US House of Representatives, 1865–7
Governor of Ohio, 1868–72 and 1876–7
Presidential annual salary: $50,000
Political party: Republican
Died: 17 January 1893, Fremont, Ohio

Above: Hayes, who had a distinguished military and political career, worked to restore the presidency's prestige, despite the controversy surrounding his election.

federal House of Representatives after the war. He resigned in 1867 to serve two terms as governor of Ohio. In 1872, he retired temporarily from political life, before winning the Republican presidential nomination and the bitterly contested election of 1876.

RESTORATION OF TRUST
Although lacking a mandate, Hayes began to re-establish the political prestige of the presidency, which had been buffeted by Lincoln's assassination, Johnson's impeachment and Grant's incompetence. Responding to political realities in the South, where the Republicans were losing the battle to eradicate racism and establish civil rights for former slaves, Hayes formally ended reconstruction. Federal troops were withdrawn on condition that Southern Democrats pledged to preserve black voting rights. The 'party of Lincoln' retreated with the troops and Democrats dominated Southern politics well into the 20th century.

LUCY HAYES
The first president's wife to have a college degree, Lucy Webb was born in Ohio in 1831 and married Hayes in 1852. Despite his controversial election, she was a popular first lady. She died in 1889.

Hayes supported the USA's return to the Gold Standard (by which the dollar was supported by the guarantee that it was convertible to a fixed weight of gold), predicting correctly that it would help to revive the economy. After the Democrats won control of Congress in 1878 he won a constitutional battle to preserve the executive's veto power over legislation. In 1880, he became the first president to visit America's west coast while in office.

Hayes honoured his pledge to serve only one term. He died in 1893. His funeral procession was led by Grover Cleveland, the president elect, along with William McKinley, then governor of Ohio, who had served in Hayes's regiment during the Civil War.

THE GOLD STANDARD
To help finance the Civil War the government began printing dollar notes, known as 'greenbacks', in 1862 and established a national currency. How to deal with the inflationary pressures this produced provoked bitter post-war arguments. The Greenback party favoured expanding the currency. Advocates of 'free silver' wanted a currency based on silver as well as gold, and 'goldbugs' argued for the Gold Standard: the government's guarantee that the paper money in circulation could be redeemed at a fixed value against the precious metal.

JAMES GARFIELD
1881

James Garfield was born in Ohio in 1831. An early seafaring ambition remained unfulfilled when, as a teenager, his tendency to fall off canal boats while trying to work on them led him to return home after six weeks with no more to show for his efforts than a fever. An academic life beckoned. Garfield went to the newly established Western Reserve Eclectic Institute in Hiram, Ohio, and then to Williams College in Massachusetts, graduating with honours in 1856. He returned to teach at Eclectic Institute, becoming its principal from 1857 to 1860. In 1858 he married Lucretia Rudolph, whom he had first known as a student there. Their first daughter and last-born son both died in infancy, but their eldest son survived until 1942, and four other children lived through World War II.

Not content with academic life, Garfield studied law privately and was admitted to the Ohio Bar in 1860, by which time he was already active in politics. A Republican, in 1859 he

Above: Garfield was assassinated before he could make any impact on the presidency.

became the youngest member of the Ohio State Senate. Following two years' military service as an officer during the Civil War, he was elected to the House of Representatives.

PRESIDENTIAL NOMINATION

He remained a Washington politician, rising to become House minority leader during Hayes's presidency. In 1880 the Ohio State Legislature elected him to the Senate. Later that year, at the Republican convention in Chicago, Garfield emerged as a compromise candidate and secured the presidential

nomination. In the election he beat the Democrat, Winfield Hancock, narrowly in the popular vote but convincingly in the electoral college.

Garfield was president for slightly more than six months. On 19 September 1881, he died of complications following an assassination attempt the previous July. He was a victim of the spoils system, the system of political patronage that had become entrenched in government at all levels. Charles Guiteau, a deranged and disgruntled office-seeker, whom Garfield had refused to appoint to a diplomatic post in Paris (on the basis that he was completely unqualified for it), shot the president as he prepared to leave Washington from the Baltimore and Potomac railway station. Even Alexander Graham Bell's new device – the metal detector, hastily invented for the purpose – could not trace the bullet, which was lodged in his pancreas, and his doctors failed to remove it. Garfield died from blood poisoning in the same New Jersey hospital in which his wife was then being treated for malaria.

Born: 19 November 1831, Orange, Ohio
Parents: Abram (1799–1833) and Eliza (1801–88)
Family background: Farming
Education: Williams College (1856)
Religion: Disciples of Christ
Occupation: Teacher
Military career: Major-General, Civil War
Political career: Ohio State Senate, 1859–61
US House of Representatives, 1863–80
US Senate, 1880
Presidential annual salary: $50,000
Political party: Republican
Died: 19 September 1881, Elberon, New Jersey

LUCRETIA GARFIELD

Born in 1832 in Ohio, Lucretia Rudolph married James Garfield in 1858. Of her seven children, five survived to adulthood. She was a conscientious and hospitable first lady, but was convalescing from malaria and nervous exhaustion when her husband was assassinated. She survived him by 36 years, until her death in 1918.

SPOILS SYSTEM

'To the victor go the spoils' describes the system in the United States by which a political party winning power gave government positions to its supporters, rewarding loyalty rather than appointing on merit. The drawback was that an incoming administration would be besieged by office-seekers, whose various demands it could not possibly hope to satisfy. The response to the assassination of Garfield was the passing of the Pendleton Civil Service Reform Act in 1883, establishing a Civil Service Commission that made an increasing number of federal appointments according to merit.

CHESTER ARTHUR
1881–1885

His political career was forged in the corrupt world of New York machine politics, but as president, Chester Arthur transcended his background, making honesty and integrity central to the conduct of his administration.

Chester Arthur was born in Vermont in 1829. His father was a Baptist minister and a committed abolitionist, who moved his family to New York. In 1848, Arthur graduated from Union College in Schenectady. After a few years' teaching he became a lawyer, and acted in some high-profile civil rights cases, including one leading to the desegregation of New York's streetcars. In 1859, he married Ellen Herndon. They had three children.

Arthur had relatives by marriage in the Confederacy. During the Civil War he was appointed quartermaster general of the state of New York, so did not see active service. In 1863 following the war, he resumed his law practice and became involved in politics as an influential member of the Republican party machine, working for Roscoe Conkling, the party's leader in New

York and a US senator. From 1871 to 1878 Arthur was collector of the Port of New York, a lucrative post that involved supervising the receipt of import duties. Some of the revenue was routinely diverted to the coffers of the state Republican party, which had close ties with the Customs House. During Rutherford Hayes's administration, the president eventually managed to reform the New York customs house. Conkling, who Hayes saw as a political rival in the Republican party, lost his source of patronage. Arthur was suspended from office.

In 1880, anxious to improve their prospects of winning New York, Garfield's supporters offered Arthur the vice-presidential nomination. The offer was accepted. Chester Arthur, the only Republican president in the late 19th century not to come from Ohio, was included on the party's ticket in 1880 principally because he was from New York, the state that then had the most electoral college votes.

He became president on 20 September 1881. Once again a vice president inherited the office but was never elected to it. In 1883, he signed the Pendleton Civil Service Reform

Left: As president, Arthur confounded his critics by supporting the reform of the spoils system.

Act, an attempt to insulate the federal bureaucracy from political influence. When his Tariff Commission suggested deep cutbacks in protectionist taxes, a nervous Congress failed to support it, passing a compromise 'Mongrel Tariff', which lowered duties on some items but raised them on a wide variety of manufactured goods. He was more successful in persuading Congress to fund the rebuilding of the navy and the refurbishment of the White House (by Louise Comfort Tiffany) as symbols of national power and prestige.

In 1882, he was diagnosed with Bright's Disease, a progressive illness affecting the kidneys. His condition remained unpublicized but two years later it played a part in his reluctant decision not to pursue the Republican presidential nomination. In 1886, two years after leaving the White House, Chester Arthur died in New York, at the age of 57.

Born: 5 October 1829, Fairfield, Vermont
Parents: William (1796–1875) and Malvina (1802–69)
Family background: Baptist ministry
Education: Union College (1848)
Religion: Episcopalian
Occupation: Lawyer
Military career: Brigadier general, Civil War
Political career: Vice president, 1881
Presidential annual salary: $50,000
Political party: Republican
Died: 18 November 1886, New York

ELLEN ARTHUR

Chester Arthur married Ellen Herndon in 1859. Born in Virginia in 1837, her first child died aged three, but a son named for his father and a daughter called after her mother survived to adulthood. Ellen died from pneumonia in 1880, the year before her husband became president, and he deeply mourned his loss: Arthur had a stained glass window erected in St John's Episcopal Church and a light kept burning inside so that he could see the window from his desk. Arthur's sister assumed the duties of hostess in the White House and looked after his children.

GROVER CLEVELAND

1885–1889

After five Republican presidents it was time for a change. The first Democrat to be elected since James Buchanan, in 1884 Grover Cleveland benefited not only from the party's revival in the South but also from the fact that, like his predecessor, he came from New York. His achievement remains unique: he is the only president to serve non-consecutive terms, winning back the White House in 1892 after losing his first re-election campaign four years previously.

When Cleveland was 16, his father, a Presbyterian minister, died. Cleveland supported his family, forgoing a college education, but still qualified as a lawyer. During the Civil War, in which, like others, he avoided military service by paying a substitute to fight in his place, he became a district attorney in Erie County, New York, and from 1870 to 1873 he served as its sheriff. In 1882 he embarked on his political career: in a

Below: Grover Cleveland was the only president to have a wedding at the White House, though the second to marry in office.

year he had moved from the mayor's office in Buffalo to the governor's mansion in Albany.

A Democrat populist (known to some as 'Uncle Jumbo'), with a reputation for confronting Tammany Hall's corruption, the fact that he might win New York made him an appealing choice for a party that had lost seven presidential elections in a row. In 1884 he faced the Republican, Senator James Blaine, an unpopular candidate even within his own party. During the campaign, Republican attacks on Cleveland's character centred on the possibility that he had fathered an illegitimate child. But in a close contest, his 1200-vote winning margin in New York finally broke the Republican stranglehold on the presidency.

POLITICAL UNPOPULARITY

Using his veto power liberally, Cleveland notably refused to sanction pensions for Civil War veterans. His economic policies, commitment to 'sound money', belief in the Gold Standard and tariff reduction, were politically divisive. Democrats in the South and West disagreed with his conviction that paper money should be backed by gold. Even though some within the party supported tariff reform, the president failed to provide strong leadership on this issue.

In 1886 his marriage to Frances Folsom, 27 years his junior, was a major event: the first presidential wedding in the White House. If the 1888 election

FRANCES CLEVELAND

Born Frances Folsom in 1864, she was the youngest ever first lady and survived longest after leaving the White House. She had five children. Frances died in 1947 at the age of 83.

Above: In 1888, Cleveland lost his home state and the electoral college, despite winning the popular vote.

had been decided by the popular vote, he would have won his second term then. Electoral college defeat, including the loss of New York, forced him to wait four years for the re-match.

Born: 18 March 1837, Caldwell, New Jersey
Parents: Richard (1804–53) and Anne (1806–82)
Family background: Presbyterian ministry
Education: Not formally educated
Religion: Presbyterian
Occupation: Lawyer
Military career: None
Political career: Sheriff, Erie County, New York, 1870–3
Mayor, Buffalo, New York, 1882
Governor of New York, 1883–5
Presidential annual salary: $50,000
Political party: Democrat
Died: 24 June 1908, Princeton, New Jersey

BENJAMIN HARRISON
1889–1893

Named for his great-grandfather, who had signed the Declaration of Independence, Benjamin Harrison was seven years old when his grandfather, President William Henry Harrison, died. Forty-eight years later, he entered the White House at a challenging time: political and economic turbulence had led to a succession of one-term presidencies. Harrison did not break the trend. His brief Republican interlude merely interrupted Cleveland's political tour de force.

Harrison's robust attitude to foreign affairs did not detract from the unpopularity caused by his domestic policies. He grappled with the onset of the deepest economic depression that the United States had experienced up to that time, which caused irreparable damage to his prospects for a second term and helped ensure Cleveland's triumphant return to office.

Harrison was born in Ohio in 1833, and graduated from Miami University in 1852. The following year he married

Below: Harrison fought in the Civil War, where he received rapid promotion and served with distinction.

Above: Harrison controversially approved congressional spending of a billion dollars, hoping to improve the USA's economic infrastructure.

Caroline Scott and they had three children. After qualifying as a lawyer, in 1854 he moved to Indiana. He joined the Republican party and entered politics in 1857, when he won election as attorney for the city of Indianapolis. During the Civil War he rose to become a brigadier general and was involved in Sherman's Atlanta campaign.

In 1876 Harrison lost an election for state governor, but four years later he entered the federal Senate. In 1888 he won the Republicans' presidential nomination and his victory in the critical swing states of New York and Indiana gave him the necessary electoral college votes to become president, despite receiving 90,000 fewer votes than Grover Cleveland. The Republicans also gained control of Congress.

SHERMAN ANTI-TRUST ACT

In terms of domestic policy, 1890 was the key year of Harrison's presidency. As well as signing into law an act providing benefits for Union veterans, he saw through the Sherman Anti-Trust Act, the first federal law of its kind

Born: 20 August 1833, North Bend, Ohio
Parents: John (1804–78) and Elizabeth (1810–50)
Family background: Farming
Education: Miami University, Ohio (1852)
Religion: Presbyterian
Occupation: Lawyer
Military career: Brigadier general, Civil War
Political career: US Senate, 1881–7
Presidential annual salary: $50,000
Political party: Republican
Died: 13 March 1901, Indianapolis, Indiana

aimed at regulating the activities of US corporations, and the Sherman Silver Purchase Act, which increased the supply of silver coinage in circulation. This backfired as the Treasury was required to buy the additional silver with notes that could be redeemed with either silver or gold: most investors demanded gold for their silver notes, causing a run on gold reserves.

BILLION DOLLAR CONGRESS

Most controversially, President Harrison supported the punitive McKinley Tariff, which imposed duties averaging more than 48 per cent on a wide range of imported goods. The tariff, which was the highest in US history, was designed to safeguard US agriculture, but it

CAROLINE HARRISON

Born in Ohio in 1832, Caroline Scott married Benjamin Harrison in 1853 and had three children, the last of whom was stillborn. She died in the White House from pneumonia in 1892.

STATES ENTERING THE UNION DURING HARRISON'S PRESIDENCY:

NORTH DAKOTA

Entered the Union: 1889

Pre-state history: Part of Louisiana Purchase (1803); organized as Dakota Territory (1861)

Total population in 1890 census: 182,719

Electoral College votes in 1892: 2

MONTANA

Entered the Union: 1889

Pre-state history: Part of Louisiana Purchase (1803); organized as Montana Territory (1864)

Total population in 1880 census: 132,159

Electoral College votes in 1892: 3

IDAHO

Entered the Union: 1889

Pre-state history: Part of Oregon and Washington Territories; organized as Idaho Territory (1863)

Total population in 1880 census: 84,385

Electoral College votes in 1892: 3

SOUTH DAKOTA

Entered the Union: 1889

Pre-state history: Part of Louisiana Purchase (1803); organized as Dakota Territory (1861)

Total population in 1880 census: 328,808

Electoral College votes in 1892: 2

WASHINGTON

Entered the Union: 1889

Pre-state history: Part of Oregon country (1846); organized as Washington Territory (1853)

Total population in 1880 census: 349,390

Electoral College votes in 1892: 4

WYOMING

Entered the Union: 1890

Pre-state history: Part of Louisiana Purchase (1803), Oregon country (1846) and land acquired from Mexico (1848); organized as Wyoming Territory (1868)

Total population in 1880 census: 60,705

Electoral College votes in 1892: 3

---

had the effect of raising prices sharply all round and in its wake caused widespread economic hardship.

Republicans dominated the 'Billion Dollar Congress', so-called because of its lavish spending plans, which cost the party much public support. In November 1890, the Democrats regained control of the House of Representatives in the mid-term elections, weakening Harrison's position within his own party.

With his secretary of state James Blaine, Harrison pursued an activist foreign policy: threatening war against Chile and standing firm in diplomatic confrontations with European powers. He supported the annexation of Hawaii when its monarchy was overthrown and a republic set up in 1893, but the treaty he put forward was later withdrawn by Grover Cleveland. (Hawaii eventually became a US territory in 1900.)

Harrison's wife Caroline died during his unsuccessful re-election campaign. After leaving office, he married Mary Dimmick, his first wife's niece, with whom he had a daughter. He became a well-regarded elder statesman, and died in 1901 in Indianapolis.

THE CHICAGO WORLD'S FAIR

1893

On 1 May 1893 President Grover Cleveland opened the Chicago World Exposition, marking the 400th anniversary of the discovery of America. Due to construction delays it was a year late, but that seemed scarcely to matter. The thousands gathered on the 240ha (600 acre) site at Jackson Park near Lake Michigan were the first who would see the attractions before the World's Fair closed almost six months later.

Chicago had beaten off challenges from St Louis, New York and Washington DC to host the event. The fair became a showcase for the city as well as for the United States. Other nations were represented there, but it was the sheer scale of the American achievement in creating the White City that housed the exhibition halls that captured the public imagination. In addition, there was Midway Plaisance, the prototype amusement park that would influence successors from Coney Island in New York to Disneyland.

A CELEBRATION

For many visitors the sight of an electric light bulb was a novelty, but other potential applications of electricity were more amazing still in household appliances such as irons and sewing machines. An early version of a fax machine was on display, and Alexander Bell's telephone company demonstrated the potential of long-distance calls between Chicago and New York. In addition to his phonographs, Thomas Edison presented a new invention, the kinetograph, which impressed his audiences with short moving picture shows.

Lectures were organized as part of the programme of events. A future president, Woodrow Wilson, delivered one. So too did the historian, Frederick Jackson Turner. His talk, 'The Significance of the Frontier in American History', became the most influential

interpretation of America's past, linking the experience of settlement with the development of national identity. Turner argued that life on the frontier shaped the American character. As a reminder of the expansion across the continent, as they left, the crowds could visit Buffalo Bill's Wild West.

The Chicago World's Fair was a visible sign of the USA's growing self-confidence and sense of its potential achievement. Barely a century old, the

Above: The Chicago World's Fair was visited by more than 27 million people.

United States was still recovering from the Civil War that had threatened its existence as a federal democratic republic. Its history had been one of territorial expansion. Economic growth, industrialization and increasing urbanization had changed the face of society as the population spread throughout the continental United States.

GROVER CLEVELAND
1893–1897

By the time Grover Cleveland returned to the White House in 1893, the first of his five children had been born, and two more daughters were born while he was president. His second inauguration took place two weeks before his 56th birthday. He had won the election convincingly, despite the impact of the Populist Party – which won 22 electoral college votes in six states – on the result. Cleveland inherited an economy that was heading into recession, and it was this situation that determined the fortunes of his second administration.

DOMESTIC CRISIS

In 1894, almost one in five of the US workforce was unemployed. Cleveland's forceful intervention in the 'Pullman strike' on the Chicago railroad lost him support among Northern workers. His repeal of the Sherman Silver Purchase Act, which he argued had helped to cause the economic depression, alienated Democrats in the South and the West, who had seen agricultural prices

Right: Rioters burn rolling stock in the strikes of 1894. The president called in the infantry to end the strikes.

Left: Cleveland's second term in office began with a financial panic on the stock exchange.

rise as a result of the inflationary pressures the Act had caused. Cleveland's continued determination to maintain the Gold Standard, the basis of 'sound money', led him to rely on J. P. Morgan to broker the necessary deals, leaving him open to the criticism that he was a puppet of Wall Street financiers. The 1894 mid-term elections were a predictable disaster for the Democrats: their only electoral support came from the Deep South.

In foreign policy, Cleveland did not intervene when Cuba rebelled against Spanish imperial control, and he reversed Harrison's policy in favour of annexing Hawaii. Where he did exert US power it was in support of the precepts of the Monroe Doctrine: threatening war in order to force Britain to accept an arbitrated solution in a boundary dispute with Venezuela.

Cleveland ended his second term deeply unpopular within his own party and in the nation as a whole. He took no part in the 1896 presidential campaign, in which the Democrats chose the populist candidate William

STATES ENTERING THE UNION UNDER CLEVELAND'S PRESIDENCY: UTAH

Entered the Union: 1896
Pre-state history: Acquired from Mexico (1848); organized as Utah Territory (1850)
Total population in 1880 census: 210,779
Electoral College votes in 1896: 3

Jennings Bryan and lost the White House to the Republicans and William McKinley.

In 1908, he died. Throughout his career in public service he had set great value on his reputation for integrity and political independence. His last words were a plea for understanding: "I have tried so hard to do right."

THE DEVELOPMENT OF NEWSPAPERS

During the 19th century the newspaper industry in the United States expanded rapidly, helped by new technologies including the steam press and the telegraph. News agencies such as Associated Press gathered and distributed news with increasing efficiency, both nationally and internationally: Britain, for example, first became aware of Abraham Lincoln's assassination in 1865 from reports carried in London by the Reuters News Agency. After the Civil War, two American newspaper tycoons came to dominate national headlines: Joseph Pulitzer and Randolph Hearst.

JOSEPH PULITZER

Born in Mako, Hungary in 1847, Pulitzer emigrated to the United States in 1864, seeking a military career, and served in the final year of the Civil War. He launched his career as a reporter on a German language paper in St Louis, which had a large German-American community, and in 1879 he became sole proprietor of a daily paper. In 1877 he married Kate Davis, a niece of the former president of the Confederacy.

In 1883 Pulitzer bought the *New York World* from Jay Gould, and set about increasing its circulation by combining news and sensational stories with serious crusades against corporate excesses and abuses of political power. He was elected to Congress as a Democrat but served only a year, resigning to concentrate on his newspaper business.

Overwork led to ill health and at the age of 40, he lost his sight. When eventually he gave up managing newspapers, he became a philanthropist, establishing the prizes for journalistic and literary achievement that are still associated with his name. In 1911, he died on board the yacht he had named *Liberty*: arriving a penniless immigrant, he had achieved the 'American Dream'.

RANDOLPH HEARST

Born into a wealthy Californian family in 1863, Randolph Hearst studied journalism at Harvard, returning home to publish his father's newspaper, the *San Francisco Examiner*, which he transformed into a popular success by modelling it on Pulitzer's *New York World*. In 1895 he acquired the *New York Morning Journal* and embarked on a circulation war with Pulitzer, employing the sensationalism and disregard for truth for

Above: Randolph Hearst built a newspaper empire and had hopes of becoming president of the United States.

which the term 'yellow journalism' was coined at the time. In 1898 when Frederic Remington, whom he had sent to Havana to provide pictures of rumoured Spanish atrocities, reported back that there was nothing much to sketch, Hearst, who like Pulitzer advocated American intervention in Cuba, allegedly sent him a telegram: "You furnish the pictures and I'll furnish the war."

Hearst represented the Democrats in Congress and campaigned unsuccessfully for the 1904 Democrat presidential nomination. The previous year he had married Millicent Willson, but it would be the actress Marion Davies who lived with him at San Simeon, the spectacular Californian castle he began building in 1919. The model for Orson Welles in his 1941 film *Citizen Kane*, Hearst died in 1951. His media empire survives.

Left: Newspapers revolutionized communication, and better transport links ensured their speedy distribution.

WILLIAM McKINLEY

1897–1901

By the end of the century, the Republican party had strayed from its roots in the radical cause of abolitionism to become the preferred choice of those who believed that the business of the United States was business. William McKinley's election campaign in 1896 was the first in which money played a decisive role. His populist opponent, William Jennings Bryan, mixed a powerful cocktail of support among the hitherto politically dispossessed in the South and the West. In a hard-fought contest, McKinley easily outspent Bryan and won, a feat he was to repeat with slightly more ease against the same opponent four years later.

William McKinley not only announced America's arrival on the world stage as a potential rival to European imperial powers, he also helped to lay the foundations for the 20th-century development of the presidency as the focal point of the United States political system.

After an education disrupted by ill health and financial problems, the

Below: McKinley's election campaign was the most expensive of its time.

Above: McKinley presided over an era of prosperity, winning a second term before falling victim to an assassin's bullet.

18-year-old McKinley joined the Ohio Volunteers when the Civil War broke out. He served as an aide to Rutherford Hayes, seeing action at Antietam. After the war, he became a lawyer and went into Republican politics. In 1871 he married Ida Saxton. They had two daughters, who both died in childhood.

POLITICAL CAREER

In 1876 McKinley won election to the federal House of Representatives. He remained in Washington for six years. Rejected by the voters in 1882, he was re-elected two years later, spending another six years in Congress until swept away in the mid-term Democrat landslide during the administration of his political mentor, President Hayes. McKinley returned to Ohio and in 1891 became governor. By 1896 he was the front-runner for the Republican presidential nomination. Helped by his campaign manager, Mark Hanna, a businessman from Ohio, McKinley was chosen as his party's candidate on the first ballot at the Republican convention in St Louis.

His election looked doubtful. The Democrats, strengthened by the support of the Populist party, had a potentially winning electoral college coalition in the South and West and a formidable candidate: William Jennings Bryan. On the principal political issue of the day – preserving the currency based on gold, or increasing the money supply by allowing the coinage of 'free silver' – Bryan was in no doubt. His appeal not to "crucify mankind on a cross of gold" was echoed by many ordinary voters.

The prospect that Bryan would become president both shocked and galvanized the business community. A gold-backed currency favoured industrial interests in the north-east and the developing cities of the Midwest. Silver inflation might appeal to the agricultural producers of the South and West but could cause financial instability. Business favoured McKinley, and money assumed its central role in presidential elections. Mark Hanna was able to raise $7 million in contributions; Bryan, with only $300,000 to spend, and despite more vigorous campaigning, was comprehensively defeated.

Born: 29 January 1843, Niles, Ohio
Parents: William (1807–92) and Nancy (1809–97)
Family background: Iron manufacturing
Education: Allegheny College
Religion: Methodist
Occupation: Lawyer
Military career: Major, Civil War
Political career: US House of Representatives, 1877–91
Governor of Ohio, 1892–6
Presidential annual salary: $50,000
Political party: Republican
Died: 14 September 1901, Buffalo, New York

Above: With a successful term in office behind him, McKinley won the election of 1900 comfortably.

THE US GOES TO WAR

Although as a Republican McKinley was firmly identified with business interests, he also courted labour leaders, appointing some to positions in his administration. But the key to rallying national support lay in his decision to go to war. As president, he flexed the USA's military muscle overseas: the Spanish–American War would bring the United States an empire of its own, in the Philippines, and also Cuba, closer to home and long coveted.

On 15 February 1898, the US battleship *Maine* exploded in Havana harbour. Though probably an accident, the US took it to be an act of provocation by the Spanish, who were then fighting against Cuban revolutionaries supported by US interests. On 23 April, with McKinley's diplomacy exhausted, Spain declared war on the United States: two days later, Congress reciprocated. It was over by December. Cuba gained a form of independence: it would be under US military occupation until 1902 and a protectorate until 1934. In addition to acquiring Puerto Rico and Guam, the United States bought the Philippines for $20 million. The investment immediately turned sour, as a nationalist insurgency there involved the USA in another four years of fighting.

In 1896 gold had been discovered in the Klondike. Prospectors rushed to Alaska and the Yukon and the first shipments arrived in the United States the following year. The production of gold doubled during the 1890s, undermining the argument for 'free silver'. In 1900, McKinley committed the United States to the Gold Standard.

Later that year he was re-elected, again beating William Jennings Bryan, this time by an even greater margin. His vice president, Garret Hobart, had died in 1899. In his place, the Republican nominee was the governor of New York: Theodore Roosevelt.

END OF AN ERA

On 6 September 1901 McKinley travelled to Buffalo, New York, to attend the Pan-American Exposition. As he shook hands with well-wishers, he was shot at close range by Leon Czolgosz, an anarchist. Despite initial optimism that he would recover, eight days later he died at the age of 58. The last chief executive elected in the 19th century, McKinley was the first 20th-century president to be assassinated. He was succeeded by Theodore Roosevelt.

Below: McKinley was shot twice, but doctors never retrieved the second bullet.

IDA McKINLEY

Ida Saxton was born in 1847 and married William McKinley in 1871. Her health deteriorated after her marriage and she suffered from epilepsy. Devoted to her husband, she survived for six years after his assassination, dying in 1907 in her birthplace of Canton, Ohio.

THE SPANISH–AMERICAN WAR
1898

John Hay, writing to his friend Theodore Roosevelt, called it a "splendid little war". As Abraham Lincoln's secretary almost 40 years previously, during a far more dramatic conflict, he was well placed to pass judgement. Following the Spanish and US declarations of war in April 1898, the fighting lasted less than four months. A peace treaty was concluded by the end of the year. US combat fatalities amounted to fewer than 400, although disease and illness killed more than ten times that number.

By the 1890s, Spain's empire in the Caribbean and the Pacific was crumbling. In Cuba and the Philippines, leaders such as Jose Marti and Emilio Aguinaldo fought against increasing Spanish repression. US sympathy for these independence movements was fuelled by humanitarian concerns, missionary fervour and the popular press. There was also a strategic motive: those in favour of US expansion overseas argued that establishing bases in the Caribbean, the Philippines and Hawaii

Above: 'Remember the Maine' became a popular slogan after its sinking precipitated war.

would protect the trading interests of the United States. While Republicans favoured annexing Hawaii, President Grover Cleveland disagreed. It was left to McKinley to approve such action during the war with Spain, giving the United States a permanent naval base at Pearl Harbor.

Below: The Spanish fleet (in the distance) was systematically destroyed by the superior US navy at the Battle of Santiago de Cuba.

After the sinking of the *Maine* in February 1898, Roosevelt, then assistant secretary to the navy, issued orders to the Pacific fleet to prepare for hostilities. The first action of the war took place at sea on 1 May: Commodore George Dewey destroyed the Spanish fleet in Manila Bay. In August, the main US invasion force reached the islands. Neither the United States nor Spain wanted Filipino independence. The day after a truce had been signed in Washington DC, a battle was engineered to keep insurgents from taking power. The Spanish surrendered and the Americans occupied Manila, but the subsequent insurrection, led by Aguinaldo, would last another four years and cost almost 4,500 American lives.

CUBA AND EXPANSIONISM

In Cuba, Roosevelt and the 'Rough Riders', the volunteer cavalry that he had helped to organize, took part in the assault on San Juan Hill on 1 July. It made him a national hero. Two days later the US navy sank enemy ships in the harbour of Santiago de Cuba, and on 17 July the remaining Spanish forces there surrendered. After the war, US forces continued to occupy the island. In 1902, the United States recognized limited Cuban independence. The following year, a treaty with the new Cuban government gave the United States a base on the island at Guantanamo Bay.

The United States, having proclaimed its support for those resisting European imperialism, had now replaced Spain as the dominant power in the Caribbean and the Pacific. Some leading Americans, including Mark Hanna, Andrew Carnegie and Mark Twain, opposed what they saw as an

Above: A general explosion ripped through the front section of the Maine, *killing more than 270 men.*

imperial adventure. For Twain, the "Person Sitting in the Darkness" would conclude that "There must be two Americas: one that sets the captive free, and one that takes a once-captive's new freedom away from him, and picks a quarrel with him with nothing to found it on; then kills him to get his land."

The Philippines provided a base for increased trade in the Far East. In 1899, John Hay, now McKinley's secretary of state, announced the 'Open Door' policy, which attempted to preserve the USA's commercial interests while the European powers and Japan sought to consolidate their influence in China. During the Boxer Rebellion the United States joined an international military force to relieve the siege of diplomatic legations in Beijing.

There were other considerations. Missionaries had long seen the religious enlightenment of the Chinese as their greatest challenge; US business interests had different ambitions. John D.

Rockefeller's company wanted to provide oil for every lamp in China.

Marti died during the Cuban struggle against Spain. Aguinaldo lived to see Philippine independence, dying in Manila in 1964. America's "splendid little war" gave Roosevelt the opportunity to use his reputation as a military hero to advance his political career, first

as governor of New York, and then as McKinley's vice president. Just over three years after fighting his way up San Juan Hill, an assassin's bullet would take him to the White House.

Below: The Rough Riders were one of three volunteer cavalries raised for the war, and the only one that saw action.

INDEX

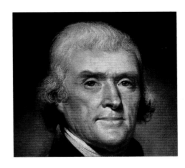

Thomas Jefferson

James Monroe

The Supreme Court

John Quincy Adams

The Capitol

The White House

Zachary Taylor